COUNSELING ASIAN FAMILIES FROM A SYSTEMS PERSPECTIVE

Edited by Kit S. Ng

THE FAMILY PSYCHOLOGY AND COUNSELING SERIES

AMERICAN
COUNSELING
ASSOCIATION

■ ■ ■

Developed Collaboratively by the American Counseling Association and
the International Association of Marriage and Family Counselors

COUNSELING ASIAN FAMILIES FROM A SYSTEMS PERSPECTIVE

10 9 8 7 6 5 4 3 2 1

American Counseling Association
5999 Stevenson Avenue
Alexandria, VA 22304

Director of Acquisitions
Carolyn Baker

Director of Publishing Systems
Michael Comlish

Copyeditor
Wendy Lieberman

Cover design by Martha Woolsey

Library of Congress Cataloging-in-Publication Data

Counseling Asian families from a systems perspective/edited by
Kit S. Ng.
   p. cm.
     Includes bibliographical references.
     ISBN 1-55620-203-2 (alk. paper)
     1. Asian American families—Mental health. 2. Asian American
families—Counseling of. 3. Family psychotherapy. I. Ng, Kit S.
RC451.5.A75 C68 1998
616.89'156'08995073—dc21   98-36526
                                                              CIP

The Family Psychology and Counseling Series

Counseling Aging Parents and Their Families
Irene Deitch, PhD, and Candace Ward Howell, MS

Counseling Asian Families From a Systems Perspective
Kit S. Ng, PhD

Counseling Families With Chronic Illness
Susan McDaniel, PhD

Mid-Life Divorce Counseling
Lita Linzer Schwartz, PhD

Social Construction in Couple and Family Counseling
John D. West, EdD, Donald L. Bubenzer, PhD, and James Robert Bitter, EdD

Transitioning From Individual to Family Counseling
Charles Huber, PhD

Understanding Stepfamilies: Implications for Assessment and Treatment
Debra Huntley, PhD

In Preparation

African American Family Therapy
Jo-Ann Lipford Sanders, PhD, and Carla Bradley, PhD

Ethical Casebook for the Practice of Marriage and Family Counseling
Patricia Stevens, PhD

Feminist Family Therapy
Kathleen May, PhD

Techniques in Couple and Family Therapy, Volume 1
Richard E. Watts, PhD

Techniques in Couple and Family Therapy, Volume 2
Richard E. Watts, PhD

Advisory Board

■■■
THE FAMILY PSYCHOLOGY AND COUNSELING SERIES

Table of Contents

PART II. COUNSELING ASIAN FAMILIES

PART III. SPECIAL ISSUES

From the Series Editor

The more you know the less you
understand. —*Tao Te Ching*

The lives of our clients are shaped by the ethnic cultures in which they live and from which their ancestors have come. Cultures determine the skills that parents think their children need to be successful; the criteria that parents use to assess the success and ability of their children; the values and child-rearing practices that parents consider to be effective, appropriate, and acceptable; and the responses that parents think their children should have to various social stimuli (Uba , 1994). Studies show that people from different cultures differ in the following:

1. The experience of pain
2. What they label as a symptom
3. How they communicate about the pain or symptoms
4. Their beliefs about cause
5. Their attitudes toward helpers (doctors and therapists)
6. The treatment they desire or expect (McGoldrick, Giordano, & Pearce, 1996, p. 9)

In this monograph we have the opportunity to learn about different Asian cultures. We will learn how their family dynamics and child-rearing practices affect values, attitudes, personality development, styles of interacting, and a host of other interpersonal factors. For example, members of traditional Asian American families are expected to adhere to their relatively clearly defined, specific position in the family hierarchy that is based on age and gender. Notably, the older and male family members have the positions of respect and power. The women have the responsibility of the emotional well-being of the family. Generally, the family exerts a lot of control over its members, and the communication patterns are hierarchial from parents down to children.

On the surface, it does not seem that the family structure is too different from a Euro-American referent group. The difference seems to be more in degree than in actual direction. Differences are seen among Euro-Americans and the various Asian American subcultures (i.e., Chinese, Filipino, Japanese, Korean, or Samoan) in expression of emotion, communication style, conformity, supervision, achievement, and social control (i.e., guilt or shame, social isolation, or physical punishment; Uba, 1994). The truth seems to be that there is no single Asian culture any more than there is one European culture. There does, however, seem to be enough difference from Euro-American families to take a special look at this group of cultures and the special treatment implications that are called for when working with them.

Dr. Ng and his collaborators do a good job of highlighting the heterogenous groups and their diversity of educational, political, socioeconomic, and religious backgrounds. For me, the importance of this monograph is the presentation of culturally relevant treatment strategies.

—*Jon Carlson, PsyD, EdD*
Series Editor

References

McGoldrick, M., Giordano, J., & Pearce, J. K. (Eds.). (1996). *Ethnicity and family therapy* (2nd ed.). New York: Guilford Press.

Uba, L. (1994). *Asian Americans: Personality patterns, identity, and mental health.* New York: Guilford Press.

Preface

Until the past decade, family therapy with Asian Americans has been one of the unexplored modalities of treatment. The landmark book by the late Dr. Man Keung Ho, *Family Therapy With Ethnic Minorities*, published in 1987, paved the way for mental health professionals who were interested in family therapy with Asian Americans to seriously consider systemic approaches as viable ways of working with Asian families. The systemic approaches seem to make sense because Asians highly value the family as a timeless institution. The idea here is to capitalize on the family as a powerful resource to bring about change. For a long time, much of the interest and writing on Asian Americans had been primarily on academic achievement, acculturation, and immigration issues. The family has seldom been involved in treatment. This "untapped" resource was a concern for my colleagues and me. We feel that when members of Asian family are committed to treatment they can become a powerful catalyst to reduce the symptoms presented by the client, resulting in significant change. With this in mind, our primary focus in this book goes beyond the individual approach in counseling. We try to broaden the context of treatment involving the family with care and respect. In a bigger context, we write with the understanding that we are dealing with "diversity within diversity" when we consider Asian cultures. In this area, the contributors' backgrounds help to create themes that connect with each other meaningfully. In spite of our efforts, we still feel that there are many areas in Asian family studies that we have yet to explore.

It is impossible not to write about Asian families in America with-out making references to families in Asia. They provide a point of reference and comparison. These "old" (families in Asia) and "new"(families in America) concepts feed on each other in a recur-sive manner.

One of our goals for this book was to make it as practical and useful as possible for clinicians. It is composed of three major parts. The first part provides a foundational framework for understand-ing Asian families. The three chapters detail vital issues of under-standing, such as cultural values, theoretical approaches, and assessment. The second part addresses challenging issues related to intervention techniques and treatment contexts. Numerous tech-niques, ranging from traditional systemic to postmodern approaches, are addressed. Case studies and practical insights from the contributor's own clinical experience are also highlighted. The third part deals with ongoing issues in the Asian community, primarily in America. Discussing issues such as homosexuality will, we hope, provide helpful information to clinicians who work with these "in-visible" clients. Insoo Berg's ideas and collaboration are both chal-lenging and timely, which is very fitting for the concluding chapter.

Last but not least, I want to thank all of the contributors for their courage to go beyond their cultural norms and write so freely about their ideas and experiences. It is my hope that this book will be-come a valuable resource to many who seek to understand and work with Asian families, both here and overseas.

—*Kit S. Ng, PhD*

Biographies

Kit S. Ng, PhD, is on the faculty of the Department of Psychology at Kean University, Union, New Jersey. He also serves as Adjunct Clinical Supervisor at the Eastern Baptist Theological Seminary in Philadelphia. Besides being a Licensed Marriage and Family Therapist–Supervisor (TX) and Licensed Professional Counselor–Supervisor (TX), he is also a Clinical Member and an Approved Supervisor with the American Association for Marriage and Family Therapy (AAMFT).

Dr. Ng received his BSc from the University of Montevallo, his MEd from the University of North Texas, and his PhD from Texas Woman's University. He has written and coauthored several articles and served as an editorial board member for several journals. He is an active member of ACA, the International Association of Marriage and Family Counselors (IAMFC), and AAMFT and is the former Regional Director of the Pennsylvania Association for Marriage and Family Therapy. Dr. Ng's research interests are in international family therapy development, treatment outcomes, supervision, and Zen psychotherapy. He also enjoys conducting cross-cultural trips for students and professionals, primarily in Asia.

Jon Carlson, PsyD, EdD, is Distinguished Professor at Governors State University in University Park, Illinois, and Director of the Lake Geneva Wellness Clinic in Wisconsin. He is the editor of *The Family Journal: Counseling and Therapy for Couples and Families* and has served as president of IAMFC.

Contributors

Teresa Hung-Hsiu Chang, MS, is a doctoral candidate in the Family Therapy Program at Texas Woman's University, Denton, Texas.

Gong Chen, EdD, is an Associate Professor in the Human Performance Department and Assistant Director of the Center of International Sport and Human Performance, San Jose State University, San Jose, California.

David S. Chou is a Master of Science candidate and graduate assistant in the Department of Counseling and Psychological Services, Georgia State University, Atlanta, Georgia.

Y. Barry Chung, PhD, is an Assistant Professor of Counseling and Psychological Services, Georgia State University, Atlanta, Georgia.

Rocco A. Cimmarusti, LCSW, is Coordinator of social welfare programs, The Family Institute at Northwestern University, and Lecturer in the Department of Education and Social Policy.

Xiaolu Hu, PhD, is an Associate Professor of Counselor Education, San Jose State University, San Jose, California.

Motoni Katayama, EdM, is a doctoral candidate in counseling psychology at the University of Illinois at Urbana—Champaign.

Annie Lau, MD, FRCP, is a Consultant in Child and Adolescent Psychiatry, Redbridge Child and Family Consultation Centre and King George Hospital, Ilford, England.

Walter Nguyen, PhD, is Executive Director of the East Dallas Counseling Center, Dallas, Texas.

Winston Seegobin, PsyD, is an Assistant Professor of Psychology in the Behavioral Science Department, Messiah College, Grantham, Pennsylvania.

Sung Ja Song, PhD, is a Professor of Social Work, Department of Social Welfare, Kyonggi University, Korea, and was Visiting Professor at the University of Chicago when she wrote her paper.

Takeshi Tamura, MD, MSc, is a Lecturer on the Faculty of Education, Tokyo Gakugei University, Nukuikita-Machi, Koganei, Tokyo.

Shi-Juian Wu, PhD, Approved Supervisor, AAMFT, Assistant Professor in Marriage and Family Therapy Program, Department of Child Development and Family Relations, East Carolina University, Greenville, North Carolina.

Ruth L. Yeh, MA, is a Multicultural Specialist in private practice in Houston, Texas; a Service Provider for Child Protective Services; and a Supervisor and Mentor for graduate students.

Muriel M. Yu, PhD, is an Associate Professor of social work, University of Texas at Arlington, and a Licensed Advanced Practitioner with a private practice in Fort Worth, Texas.

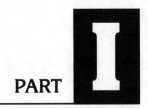

PART **I**

UNDERSTANDING AND ASSESSING ASIAN FAMILIES

1

Theoretical Framework for Therapy With Asian Families

Teresa Hung-Hsiu Chang, MS
Ruth L. Yeh, MA

Ethnic families in America are extremely diverse. Counselors working with families of minority ethnic groups need to take into consideration how values, beliefs, and assumptions within ethnic cultures have an impact on family dynamics. Counselors also need to be aware that their own cultural background may influence their therapeutic strategies in working with these families (Lum, 1986). Therefore, counselors should acknowledge cultural differences and the value of different cultural practices.

It cannot be assumed that the frame of reference for counseling Asian families is the same as it is for White, middle-class, American families. Many important cultural themes might be potentially ignored in the process of therapy with Asian American families. The cultural and economic transition of moving into a new country has been accomplished at times with success, but more frequently with conflict and alienation. During the transition, Asian American families' language, customs, beliefs, and structure began to shift and change, and these changes have major emotional and psychological consequences with which they must continue to grapple.

It is necessary to construct a culturally related theoretical framework for therapy with families of minorities. Moreover, counselors need to consider whether families from a particular culture require a particular style of family therapy. The fit between various psychotherapies and culture is crucial to the success of counseling (Ho, 1987; McGoldrick, Pearce & Giordano, 1982).

Family Systems Theory

System family therapy derives its underlying conceptual framework from systems theory. Its premise is that individual dysfunction is understood and changed within the family system. Indeed, system family therapists believe that individual dysfunction is an aspect of systems dysfunction, and the family system is the fundamental unit for intervention. General system theory is most often associated with the work of von Bertalanffy (1968), in which all living things are viewed as open systems and best understood by an examination of the interrelationships among components. Therapists operating from a general systems framework conceptualize the family as an open system that evolves over the family life cycle in a sociocultural context. Consequently, the word *system* is also linked to different ethnic and cultural contexts.

Family therapists stress the idea that the family is a whole and that a change in one member's functioning affects all other members. Furthermore, causes and effects are circular rather than linear, and interventions into any part of the system affect the whole system. Most system family therapists aspire to rise above the limits of the linear model of thinking that is necessary for acquiring a systemic view of the transactions of client families. In brief, it is vital for counselors to comprehend the basic features of systems theory: It devotes attention to the whole, to the transactional process among the units of system, to the ongoing processes of information and feedback loops, and to repeated interactions and patterns inherent to the family system (Minuchin, 1974).

Bowenian Family Therapy

Murray Bowen's focus has primarily been with the multigenerational family system. Through clinical studies, Bowen noticed that the ego boundaries between schizophrenic family members connected one generation to the next (McGoldrick & Gerson, 1985). Bowen (1978) introduced the "three-generation hypothesis" of schizophrenia to explain the way families transmit themes and patterns over generations. Marital patterns, other family relationships, and psychopathology are often transmitted over several generations in a family. For example, one can usually trace alcoholism over at least three generations.

According to Bowen, the major problem in families is emotional fusion, and thus the major goal of therapy is to increase differentiation. A differentiated person can stay in contact with family members and maintain his or her own integrity without fear of becoming fused into the family's emotional mass (Guerin & Penddagast, 1976). The higher the level of one's differentiation, the more distinguishable his or her emotional and intellectual systems. This means that the differentiated person is nonreactive, whereas the undifferentiated person is reactive to anxiety and stress. Continued lack of differentiation in the family may result in marital conflict, dysfunction in one spouse, or impairment of one or more children. On the contrary, the healthy family can remain in viable emotional contact from one generation to another.

Bowen (1978) postulated that when anxiety arises in a relationship, people frequently create triangles to diffuse that anxiety and stabilize the relationship. When anxiety increases between two family members, a vulnerable third person is predictably and automatically involved in the emotional issue. For example, one parent and a child can form a triangle against the other parent, or parents can align against a child. Bowen found that helping adult family members differentiate from their own families of origin often has positive effects on the clients relationships with their spouses and children. His findings have led to the use of family-of-origin procedures as the treatment of choice for many family problems (McGoldrick & Gerson, 1985).

A critical goal of Bowenian family therapy is to help the clients respond to family members by becoming less reactive. Another important goal of therapy is to increase the degree to which one is able to distinguish between the feeling process and the intellectual process. These goals are largely accomplished by genograms and assignments. To promote the goal, the therapist acts as a coach, which helps increase differentiation by asking different process questions (Bowen, 1978). In addition, the therapist encourages clients to begin a lifelong effort of self-discovery.

Bowenian family therapy has important implications for Asian American families. The emphasis on intergenerational dynamics by Bowen fits the Asian family tree. Within Asian American families, it is culturally acceptable to have three generations living together. Thus, a mother–child–grandmother triangle, as well as the mother-in-law–husband–wife triangle, can be an occurring pattern along with other issues. The Bowenian family therapist can coach family members in detriangulating, after which the emotional system of the family can be modified. Instead of honoring individualism, most Asian Americans define and value the "self" within the context of family relationship. Consequently, the differentiation process enables clients to obtain balance between the power of the individual and that of the family.

Becoming a well-differentiated person also helps Asian Americans make cultural adjustments to the larger social and cultural context, which tends to be very individualistic. Because of the Asian tradition of valuing authority, the expert role and coaching style of the therapist in this model fit the Asian client's expectation of a helping professional. This allows the Asian American family to easily adapt to the role of client and possibly make appropriate changes in therapy. The flexibility of Bowen's approach to seeing different family members at different times seems to be very adaptive to most Asian families. This prevents family members from disclosing personal issues in front of other family members. The clients will not feel threatened with losing face, and the dignity of individuals might be secured (Ho, 1987). In brief, Bowenian family therapy provides the mental health professional with a transgenerational perspective and differentiation orientation that works well with Asian American families. These assets promote balance for some Asian American families struggling between their cultural entity and Western lifestyle.

Structural Family Therapy

Salvador Minuchin was trained as a pediatrician in Argentina and later trained as a psychiatrist in the United States in the 1950s. He started developing his theory, techniques, and action-oriented intervention from the experience of working with the children and adolescents of poor and disorganized families living in the ghetto. In this model, the family is viewed as a social system, and patterns of repeated interactions underpin that system (Minuchin, 1974). Structural family therapists change the structures underlying the system through modifying family interactions. The interactions and transactions inherent in the family system are guided by boundaries that define, maintain, and modify rules of the family (Minuchin & Fishman, 1981). Healthy boundaries protect the autonomy of individuals and subsystems. Unhealthy boundaries show the rigid or diffuse boundaries within disengaged or enmeshed families. Accordingly, it is essential for the structural family therapist to observe the family system and promote an effective hierarchical structure.

Each family system includes subsystems, such as spousal or sibling groups. Subsystems carry out specialized functions and promote the wholeness of the overall system. Therefore, the structural family therapist cannot intervene in one part of the family system without taking the others into account (Minuchin, 1974). For example, instead of being labeled as an adolescent's symptomatic behavior, anorexia nervosa can be a diagnosis of the family system from the perspective of structural therapy. In this case, the structural family therapist helps each family member take responsibility for causing and maintaining the syndrome and for changing the organization of family.

Each family has its own preferred steady state (homeostasis) that is protected by the system. To change the established homeostatic patterns and gain entrance to the system, Minuchin developed techniques of joining that effectively enable the therapist to be accepted as a "distant relative" (Minuchin, 1974). As a means to restructure the family system, the therapist assesses the transactions and boundaries of the system and formulates the interventions, such as confronting and challenging the family. Minuchin has sometimes increased the stress or created a crisis within the family for the purposes of unbalancing family homeostasis. By creating a family crisis, he forces the family to change the system and substitute a more functional state of interrelating, and the family structure can be transformed (Nichols & Schwartz, 1995).

Structural family therapy provides a culturally flexible framework for effectively understanding and intervening in Asian American families. The flexibility of structural family therapy lies with its major emphasis on the family as a boundary-maintaining social system in constant transition with its immediate social environment (Ho, 1989). Family therapy guided by this framework formulates interventions that help families maintain healthy boundaries that adapt to cultural transitions and reduce destructive social and cultural impacts on the Asian American family (Minuchin, 1974). Applying structural family therapy in recently immigrated Asian American families helps them deal with stress of adjusting to the new cultural and economic environment. Moreover, the development of the family life cycle within these families is disturbed by the process of cultural transition. As a result, stress existing in the transition can be symptomatic, as well as problematic, to recent-immigrant Asian American families. In addition to the issue of transition, the different rates of acculturation in family members cause cultural value differences, which contribute to family conflicts (Hong, 1989). For example, different rates of acculturation in the parent–children subsystem might cause conflicts and stress on relationships. The structural therapist's use of joining techniques can be especially helpful in treating Asian American families. The joining technique requires the therapist to listen with empathy, genuine interest, and appropriate feedback, which promotes the process of understanding and accepting the family, as well as its presenting problem within a cultural context. On the other hand, joining is a process in which the therapist is accepted by the family as a leader, and this fits the Asian culture's tradition of hierarchy. In brief, structural family therapy provides the mental health professional an opportunity to reconstruct the hierarchy and power of families. This helps Asian American families, especially recent-immigrant families, make the transition in their new social environment.

Strategic Family Therapy

Jay Haley, a leading strategic family therapist, is well known for his problem-solving therapy (Haley, 1976). Unlike other strategic therapists, Haley bridged what he learned from three pioneers of family therapy, Milton Erickson, Gregory Bateson, and Salvador Minuchin. He incorporated Minuchin's structural conception of family organization into his application of strategic techniques. Because Haley participated in developing Bateson's "double-bind" concept in the 1950s, his strategic techniques are largely based on the communications theory of Bateson and the clinical genius of Erickson.

According to communication theory, it is the fundamental assumption of strategic therapy that communication defines the nature of the relationship one is having with a partner. Haley defined symptoms as interpersonal strategies that are used employed by one person to deal with another and to control the definition of the relationship (Haley, 1963). Therefore, the therapist needs to help the patient develop other ways of defining relationships and replace symptomatic strategies. Haley has also been concerned with the issue of power alliances and coalitions within a family, which usually present themselves in the metacommunicative aspects of family relationships. He also relabelled dysfunctional behavior as a reasonable problem-solving strategy, making it more understandable (Haley, 1963). This enables the therapist to work with the family without much resistance.

The initial goal of strategic family therapy is to resolve the presenting problem, and the ultimate goal is to organize the hierarchy and generational boundaries of family. In addition, intermediate goals emerge during the stages of therapy because, in Haley's view, families cannot move from a dysfunctional structure directly to a functional one and instead must proceed through different states (Haley, 1980). To avoid the formation of problems, as well as to eliminate symptoms, Haley's problem-centered and pragmatic approach focuses on changing behavioral sequences. He places major emphasis on the interactive processes taking place between individual family members and subsystems within the family. For this purpose, strategic family therapists take responsibility for changing the family organization and resolving the problem. The role of the therapist is defined by Haley as a "metagovernor of the family system" (Haley, 1963), and it requires intense active participation and at times manipulation. To reach the desired treatment goals, the process of therapy needs to include allowing a social encounter, defining the problem, observing the interaction of the family, clarifying desired change, and ending the interview with homework (Haley, 1976).

Instead of taking a feeling- and growth-oriented approach, strategic family therapy (Haley, 1963) emphasizes the interactive patterns in which family members influence one another's behavior, both verbally or nonverbally. This emphasis on changing the behavior of family members and the sequence of interactions seems to be applicable to most Asian American families seeking professional help, particularly with the focus on brief treatment. In addition, metacommunication, defined as communication containing information as well as a command (Sluzki, 1979; Watzlawick, Beavin, & Jackson, 1967), can be used by the mental health professional. The metacommunication within Asian American families is further complicated by the processes of immigration and acculturation, in which power structure, definition of role, family functions, and family transactions are changed. More important, the role of the therapist, as defined by Haley (1976), requires intense active participation; however, the active leadership of the therapist may easily be interpreted by Asian American families as an unwelcome intrusion (Ho, 1987). Therefore, the interventions of the therapist should be guided by thoughtfulness of the cultural values of Asian American families at the beginning stage of therapy. In brief, strategic family therapy provides the mental health professional with interventions and procedures to break the cycle of problems inherent in the interaction of Asian American families.

Solution-Focused Brief Therapy

Steve de Shazer, Insoo Kim Berg, and their associates developed the theory of solution-focused brief therapy in the Brief Family Therapy Center (BFTC) in Milwaukee during the 1970s. De Shazer synthesized theories from his earlier Eriksonian practice, concepts of Batesonian theory, and the basic tenets of the Mental Research Institution. Insoo Kim Berg has been skillful in demonstrating and providing training for this model (Nichols & Schwartz, 1995). The focus of the BFTC group is on solutions rather than the cause of the problem. Their belief is that potential interventions are easier to identify while the therapist focuses on nonproblematic behaviors (de Shazer, 1985). They also assume that the client brings complaints as well as solutions to therapy. In this model, change is viewed as inevitable and is likened to a snowball effect in which small changes lead to bigger ones. In addition, change is generated from cooperation between the clients and the therapist. To build this cooperation, the therapist should pay proper respect to the worldview of clients (de Shazer, 1985). Indeed, to respect the client is often more important than to help solve problems.

Clinically, BFTC therapists place value on creating solutions that fit in the worldview and patterns of thoughts, feelings, and behaviors of clients. In other words, therapists do not request clients to think in ways that are foreign to them (Berg, 1992). Translating this into practice, de Shazer (1985) emphasized setting goals based on the worldview of clients. A well-defined goal can transform problematic situations into clinically solvable forms. Hence, goal setting is the essential therapeutic task because it gives the therapy a focus of change, and it also enables clients to measure their progress. The therapist needs to clarify goals by imposing constructive questions, such as "How would you know things are better?" An effective goal is realistic, practical, concrete, and achievable (Berg, 1992).

After setting a goal, the therapist looks for exceptions to the problem through different techniques, such as miracle questions, scaling questions, or relationship questions (Berg & Jaya, 1993). Exceptions are those behaviors and thoughts that contrast with the complaint or problem. Exceptions to problems are incidents in which those complaints look less severe or do not exist at all for the client. Therefore, exceptions have the potential of leading to a solution if amplified by the therapist or increased by the client (de Shazer, 1991). Solution-focused brief therapists believe that exceptions are always inherent within presenting problems. Every complaint pattern includes some sort of exception—a clue for solutions. The job of the therapist is to create ways for clients to be more aware of these exceptions. Very often, the therapist asks clients to do something different because it requires them to try new behaviors (de Shazer, 1991). Once the therapist finds out what client behaviors work to solve problems, he or she encourages the client to do more of the same types of behavior. This means clients find their own solutions instead of the ones imposed by the therapist.

The following ideas suggested by solution-focused brief therapy seem to meet the needs of Asian American families within their cultural context. First, using mental health services is the last resort for most Asian American families. When they do reach out to service providers, the nature of problems tends to be crisis oriented (Berg & Jaya, 1993). Accordingly, solution-focused brief therapy redefines the nature of presenting problems by focusing on strengths. Second, instead of exploring feelings, Asian American clients expect the therapy to be brief and focused on finding solutions. Third, Asian American families also want change to be generated as soon as possible without focusing on the detailed causes of the problem. Therefore, the goal-setting process within this model respects ethnic differences in treatment (Chang, 1993).

Furthermore, the foundation of solution-focused brief therapy is to cooperate with the clients' view of the problem. Berg and Jaya (1993) believed that most Asian American clients want to cooperate with the mental health professional, but the therapist must be sensitive to the worldview and cultural value of these families to work with them effectively. In brief, solution-focused brief therapy provides the mental health professional with a model that Asian American families feel comfortable with when they are in need of therapy.

Conclusion

Asian American families are like all other families, like some other families, and like no other families. It is impossible to generalize about Asian American families because there is no "typical" Asian American family. Each Asian national group has a distinctive cultural heritage, history, and reasons for immigrating to the U.S.

(Takake, 1990). Here are some final suggestions that will, we hope, help counselors produce positive outcomes in their work with Asian American families.

First, therapists need to be aware of their own cultural values and belief system. Imposing one's values and belief system without seeking to understand the clients' would definitely hinder the effectiveness of treatment. One key element in the therapeutic process is the ability of therapists to explore their own feelings, attitudes, and stereotypes about Asian Americans (Shon & Ja, 1982). Second, different models have different focuses in working with families, but there are essentials in developing meaningful therapeutic relationships with Asian American families. According to McGill (1983), these essentials include forming the therapeutic alliance, understanding and joining families in their language and context, helping them respond to problems differently, and reaffirming their increased problem-solving strategies. In addition to understanding the presenting problems, the experiences of the family in America must be taken into account in the helping process.

Lum (1986) suggested that therapists should know the family's cultural defenses and support systems and skillfully promote the family's sense of power and competencies. More important, cultural rules relating to authority structures, differentiation, and boundaries should be acknowledged to avoid sending culturally incongruent messages to the family. For example, the therapist should confirm the parents' authority role with respect to the children while he or she joins the family. The maladaptive behavior of the identified patient often needs to be reframed as normal and intelligible in the context of family worries. In addition, it is necessary to confirm the correctness of interpretation when two languages are involved in the process.

References

Berg, I. K. (1992). *Family based service.* Milwaukee, WI: Brief Family Therapy.

Berg, I. K., & Jaya, A. (1993). Different and same: Family therapy with Asian-American families. *Journal of Marital and Family Therapy, 19,* 31–38.

Bowen, M. (1978). *Family therapy in clinical practice.* New York: Jason Aronson.

Chang, T. H. (1993). The rhythm of change: Tracing the relatedness of the solution-focused brief therapy and the I Ching in the phenomenological dimension of therapy. Unpublished master's thesis, Texas Woman's University.

de Shazer, S. (1985). *Keys to solution in brief therapy*. New York: Norton.

de Shazer, S. (1991). *Putting differences to work*. New York: Norton.

Guerin, P. J., & Penddagast, E. A. (1976). Evaluation of family system and genogram. In P. J. Guerin (Ed.), *Family therapy: Theory and practice*. New York: Gardner Press.

Haley, J. (1963). *Strategies of psychotherapy*. New York: Grune & Stratton.

Haley, J. (1976). *Problem-solving therapy*. San Francisco: Jossey-Bass.

Haley, J. (1980). *Leaving home*. New York: McGraw-Hill.

Ho, M. K. (1987). *Family therapy with ethnic minorities*. Newbury Park, CA: Sage.

Ho, M. K. (1989). Applying family therapy theories to Asian/Pacific Americans. *Contemporary Family Therapy*, *11*, 60–71.

Hong, G. K. (1989). Application of cultural and environmental issues in family therapy with immigrant Chinese Americans. *Journal of Strategic and Systemic Therapies*, *8*, 14–21.

Lum, D. (1986). *Social work practice and people of color: A process-stage approach*. Monterey, CA: Brooks/Cole.

McGill, D. (1983). Cultural concepts for family therapy. In C. J. Falicov (Ed.), *Cultural perspectives in family therapy*. Rockville, MD: Aspen.

McGoldrick, M., & Gerson, R. (1985). *Genograms in family assessment*. New York: Norton.

McGoldrick, M., Pearce, J., & Giordano, J. (1982). *Ethnicity in family therapy*. New York: Guilford Press.

Minuchin, S. (1974). *Families and family therapy*. Cambridge, MA: Harvard University Press.

Minuchin, S., & Fishman, H. C. (1981). *Family therapy techniques*. Cambridge, MA: Harvard University Press.

Nichols, M. P., & Schwartz, R. C. (1995). *Family therapy: Concepts and methods*. New York: Allyn & Bacon.

Shon, S. P., & Ja, D. (1982). Asian families. In M. McGoldrick, J. Pearce, & J. Giorddano (Eds.), *Ethnicity in family therapy*. New York: Guilford Press.

Sluzki, C. (1979). Migration and family conflict. *Family Process*, *18*, 379–389.

Takake, R. (1990). *Strangers from a different shore: A history of Asian Americans*. Boston: Little, Brown.

von Bertalanffy, L. (1968). *General systems theory*. New York: Braziller.

Watzlawick, P., Beavin, J., & Jackson, D. (1967). *Pragmatics of human communication: A study of interactional patterns, pathologies and paradoxes*. New York: Norton.

■ ■ ■

2

Multimodel Assessment of Asian Families

Muriel M. Yu, PhD

A ssessment is one of the key elements of counseling. It is a criti-cal process whereby clinicians obtain important and relevant information, formulate tentative hypothesis of the nature and extent of the client's problems, evaluate the client's motivation to make necessary changes, and decide on different effective means to achieve desirable goals mutually agreed on by client and the clinician. Because of the complexity of human condi-tions and the ever-increasing knowledge of the interrelatedness of individuals and their environment, the importance of a multi-dimensional approach to assessment that includes environmen-tal forces and impacts is widely accepted by mental health professionals. In multicultural and multiethnic practice, assess-ment must take into consideration another important factor: the cultural and ethnic background of clients. For example, the *Di-agnostic and Statistical Manual of Mental Disorders* has evolved from listing a limited medical diagnosis of psychiatric illness at its beginning to inclusion of social, functional, and cultural and ethnic considerations in its latest edition (American Psychiatric Association, 1994).

In the field of family therapy, no single systematic approach to assessment of families exists (Johnson, Rasbury, & Siegel, 1986).

Although some continue to advocate for model-specific assessment procedures from which to proceed into the corresponding treatment techniques, research also shows that particular therapeutic approaches are more likely to be effective for certain problems than for others (Garfield, 1983; Kazdin, 1988). Furthermore, most existing theories on family therapy were developed based on nonethnic samples, and their applicability to various ethnic groups have yet to be tested.

Because of increasing racial and ethnic diversity in the United States, family therapists are more aware of cultural influences on family dynamics and interactions. McGoldrick and Giodana (1996) emphasized that clients' personal contexts are largely shaped by the ethnic cultures in which they live and from which their ancestors have come. Thus, family therapists need to be knowledgeable of various cultures and their impact on working with ethnic families and develop a level of cultural competency to render more effective and relevant services to these families.

A Multimodel Assessment

Depending on the purpose and setting, various protocols are used by family therapists in making an assessment. For example, a combination of structured interview and forms that supply basic demographic data are generally used by most family service agencies. Existing standard instruments such as genogram, ecomap, Family Life Map, Family Crisis Oriented Personal Scales, Family Function Questionnaire, Family Relationship Index, and Family Strength questionnaire all give useful information in evaluating various aspects of family functions and areas of conflicts or concerns. Some of these may be useful with highly acculturated Asian American families, but the vast cultural differences between Asian and Western societies, proficiency in the English language, families' cultural identity, and other variables must be taken into consideration when making family assessments. Also to be considered are Asian family structure and communication patterns, whether members are foreign-born or U.S.-born, and immigration experience, including being a refugee. Obtaining relevant and pertinent data on all factors is the most crucial first step.

Different authors have proposed different focuses in assessing Asian American families. Shon and Ja (1982) emphasized social class, geographical origin, birthplace, and generation in the United States as key factors. Lee (1982, 1996) suggested that family composition, kinship networks, coping styles of family members, marital relations, intergenerational differences, migration history, and extent of support systems are most important. She focused on two dimensions: the internal family system, which includes the understanding of individual members and family subsystems, and external factors, which include the community and other environmental stressors. The multimodel assessment proposed here incorporates the theoretical frameworks of these authors with additional variables highlighted.

The Strength Perspective

Historically, mental health professionals have focused on clients problems and deficits and family therapists have often concentrated on the dysfunctional aspect of family interaction. Added to this historical fact is the non-Asian's stereotype of Asian families as enmeshed or isolated, which further distorts the information needed to gain understanding for the purpose of relevant and effective intervention. A strength-perspective assessment looks at Asian American families in the context of their particular cultural and ethnic strengths. Weaver (1982) stated, "It is crucial to begin with strengths of the family system: Family move on strengths, not weakness. There are inherent strengths in the design of every family" (p. 103). Many Asian cultural norms, such as support from extended family members and siblings, the strong sense of obligation, the strong focus on educational achievement, the work ethic, the high tolerance for loneliness and separation, and the loyalties of friends or between employer and employee, are distinct assets of Asian Americans (Lee, 1982). Clinicians need to recognize these positive cultural characteristics and reinforce these strengths in families when they are seemingly overwhelmed with the problems at hand. These strengths can also be used as resources for the families.

Cultural and Ethnic Identity

Ethnicity is a major form of group identification and has significant impact on values and belief systems, as well as family structure, interactions, and communication patterns. The Asian American population includes descendants of immigrants from the 1800s, as well as those who are recent immigrants or refugees. The extent to which families identify with their original ethnic group is an important area for exploration. An assumption exists that the longer any given group has resided in this country the more assimilated the group becomes. This assumption may apply only to certain European Americans and does not always apply to other ethnic groups, especially people of color. Therefore, in assessing Asian American families' cultural and ethnic identity, clinicians need to look beyond the length of residency in this country and family roots. Proficiency in the English language may or may not be an indicator of a family's ties with their cultural and ethnic origin. For instance, a recent Chinese immigrant from Hong Kong who was brought up in a highly westernized banking family but does not have a good command of English language may be more adapted to the Western culture than a second generation Chinese person who grew up in San Francisco's Chinatown where his or her parents ran a small family business. Much depends on geographic location, upbringing, educational experiences, and prior exposure to and immersion in Western culture.

When assessing family's cultural and ethnic identity, Ho's (1987) family cultural transitional map, along with ecomaps and genograms, can be used. Family members' country of origin, time of migration, birthplace, place of employment, social network, religious affiliation, social support, and other pertinent information can be added to other demographic information at the initial interview. By doing this with the whole family present, it is hoped that all family members will benefit from the recounting of their roots, traditions, and the history they share as a family. This is especially useful if children were too young when they left their homeland, and it gives parents the opportunity to share with their children some important historical data.

The culturagram by Congress (1994) is another useful tool for assessing Asian American families. In a culturagram, cultural information for a specific family can be divided into many categories. Depending on the family's situation, information can be obtained in the following categories: (a) length of time in the community; (b) spoken language, native language, English, or bilingual ability; (c) contact with cultural institutions—ethnic churches, schools, and social clubs; (d) health beliefs—native attitudes about health, illness, and treatment that differ from American medical practices; (e) holidays and special events—religious and life-cycle transitional events such as birth, marriage, and death; (f) education and work values; (g) family patterns of support; (h) crisis events and stressors; and (i) education and career selection.

Acculturation Process

All immigrants go through a process of a gradual adaptation to the cultural values, beliefs, customs, and behaviors of the new country, leaving behind the norms and behaviors from their country of origin. Because culture can be instilled in a person as early as 5 or 6 years of age, depending on when one moves to another country and new social and environmental influences, some immigrants may never adapt completely to the host culture. As a result, acquisition of a new language, identity, value and belief system, and behavior patterns is a gradual, continuous process. Biculturation may be the optimal model for cross-cultural adaptation for many immigrants (Lum, 1995).

For Asian American families, conflict may occur because of different rates of acculturation between parents and children. Because children are in the formative stages of development, they may be easily influenced by peers. They invariably surpass their parents in the rate of acquisition of the English language. They often adopt Western modes of behavior and thinking quickly and adapt to the host cultural values and practices much sooner than their parents. Parents, on the other hand, have held their cultural norms and behaviors much longer and may be less willing to replace them with new ones that may be too foreign and threatening to their identity and security. Parents lack opportunities for learning a new language or having a similar socialization process to what their children receive in school.

Because of language and other cultural barriers, some immigrant parents may depend on their children to translate and negotiate when they encounter educational, legal, or financial transactions. Thus, in addition to conflicts caused by different cultural beliefs and practices between parents and children, role reversal between parents and children pose further threats to parents' sense of authority and control.

To measure parents' and children's degree of acculturation into Western culture, Congress's (1994) culturagram can be used to assess family members' acculturation rates by asking each individual member separately questions regarding his or her length of residency in this country and degree of adaptation to the cultural norms and beliefs of the United States. Useful questions include How old were you when you came to the United States? What languages do you speak at home, at school (or work), and in the community in general? What language do you prefer to use at home or in the community? To what clubs or groups do you belong? What is your religious or spiritual belief? What church or temple do you go to? When you are sick, where do you go for treatment? To whom do you turn for help? What particular events are stressful for you? Information gained through these inquiries can help clinicians determine where individual members are in the acculturation process, the extent and nature of conflicts between parents and children, and interventions needed to resolve differences and conflicts.

Family Structure, Role Expectations, and Communications Patterns

Although Asians are known to have multigenerational family compositions, studies have shown more Asian American families in the U.S. have taken on a nuclear family structure, because of acculturation process and other practical considerations (del Carman, 1990). When compared with European American families, however, Asian American families still have a higher percentage of multigenerational households, usually with the parents of one of the spouses living with the family. The reason for many of the multigenerational households is economic as well as cultural. Adult sons and daughters show respect and fulfill their "filial piety" duty by sharing their home with their elderly parents, and parents gain a sense of usefulness by taking care of grandchildren and sharing household responsibilities, such as cooking and gardening. Conflicts arising from inevitably different acculturation rates between parents and young children are compounded when three generations are involved.

Parental role function and expectations among Asian American families pose special stresses to newly arrived immigrants. Traditional Asian families are hierarchical and patriarchal, and role functions are clearly delineated. Many new immigrant families have been labeled as "incomplete" because family members can be separated for months or years in the process of immigrating from Asia to the U.S. (Wong, 1985). Separation may have voluntary causes, such as employment and financial demands, or involuntary causes, such as immigration laws. In consideration of children's educational needs, mothers often accompany their children to the U.S. ahead of their husbands. Long separation among family members may result in emotional hardship and role adjustment. Traditional Asian family roles as prescribed by Confucianism are highly defined, hierarchical, and patriarchal, and conflicts often arise when mothers take on the discipline of children, conflicting with the traditional norms of "strict father, kind mother" role expectations.

Marital role function and expectations undergo transition as well. Contrary to the common stereotype of Asian women being subservient and obedient toward their husbands, studies show that Asian women in general are more progressive in their views regarding husband-and-wife relations than are Asian men (Chia et al., 1985). Research also indicates that Asian American women acculturate more quickly into American culture than do Asian American men (Arkoff, Meredith, & Doug, 1963). These combined factors lead Asian American women to expect a more egalitarian relationship in their marriage roles than their husbands expect. Of course, gender-based roles and expectations within marriage systems influence not only the marital relationship but also parental roles and expectations. Clinicians need to identify discrepancies between marital partners' role expectations and evaluate their capacity and willingness to modify their expectations of each other as part of family assessment.

Communication Style and Emotional Expressiveness

As a group, Asian Americans may rely on interpersonal and social cues in social interaction and show more restraint and hesitancy when communicating with family members (Hsu, Tseng, Ashton, McDermott, & Char, 1985). Strong emotional expressions are considered inappropriate, both at home and in public. Asian American families may value sharing thoughts more than sharing feelings (McDermott, Char, Hsu, Tseng, & Ashton, 1983). These communication styles can negatively impact family interactions and relationships. This is especially true if the younger generation has become "westernized" and is accustomed to direct and open expressions of feelings, but parents continue to observe the more traditional communication style. When under stress, parents may feel that openly expressing emotions such as fears or sadness can undercut their authority and bring shame on themselves. Children may balk at the thought of seeing vulnerability in their parents (Uba, 1994).

In the context of client–therapist interaction, the differences in communication styles between East and West make assessing Asian American families complex. For example, Asian American clients may expect the clinicians to pick up on subtle cues because direct form of communication, especially among strangers, is considered rude and unacceptable.

Other communication obstacles include Asian Americans' attitude toward self-disclosure. Asian culture dictates that individuals guard their privacy, especially regarding negative feelings or family problems. Many Asian American clients avoid mentioning inner feelings. Instead, they are more likely to depict events or factual information. They may analyze problems related to other people or to people in general to avoid focusing on themselves. To Asian Americans, self-disclosure not only violates the private self but is also a betrayal of one's family. That belief would generate more guilt feelings than are already present. All of these dynamics must be taken into consideration in the process of formulating a problem statement. A certain amount of prodding from the clinician may be necessary before Asian American families feel comfortable discussing the problems at hand (Uba, 1994). Even after problems are identified, a danger of misrepresentation of the extent of those problems by clients exists. That is, family members may convey their discomfort in a manner that makes a problem seem less severe so the clinician can easily underestimate the extent of the problem (Chin, 1983).

Immigration Status and Migration History

Until 1960, most Asian Americans were descendants of early Japanese and Chinese immigrants. Today, over half of Asian Americans are foreign born, and over 1 million of them are refugees from Southeast Asia who have arrived since 1975 (U.S. Department of Health and Human Services, 1993). Although refugees may share some similarities with immigrants in terms of cultural values, family traditions and structure, language, and religion, the populations differ in many other ways. First, immigrants may come to the U.S. because of attractive opportunities or possibilities of advancing their economic and career goals. Refugees, on the other hand, come to the U.S. because they were pushed out of their homeland by political upheavals and were accepted here. Second, with few exceptions, Asian immigrants have usually planned their exit from their country of origin and entry into U.S., so their settlement and transition are more orderly. Experiences for Southeast Asian refugees are tumultuous in all phases of their relocation and settlement into the U.S. All of them suffered from the cruelties of war and its aftermath. Many were tortured in prison camps or brutalized when fleeing their homeland. Finally, if they were successful in reaching safety, many of them had to remain in refugee camps for long periods of time with minimum living standards and poor health and mental health conditions. Immigrants may experience a sense of loss because of separation from family members, friends, and employment affiliation, but they still have the option or hope of maintaining contacts with the people they value. Many Asian refugees, in addition to losing personal possessions, have experienced loss of immediate and extended family members or close friends during war, in their escape safety, or in the wait at refugee camps (Lee & Oberst, 1989).

The unique traumatic experiences of Southeast Asian refugees has a significant impact on their subsequent health and mental health status and their family life. They are at high risk for mental disorders, such as depression and posttraumatic stress disorder among adults and anxiety and acting out behavior among children (Tran, 1993). Observations at public and private social service agencies indicate that child abuse and family violence may be on the increase as well. Thus, mental health professionals are more likely to see many Asian American families in their clinical setting. Clinicians must assess these families migration experiences, trauma suffered, loss of family members or close friends, prior coping skills and their success or failure, and resources or support available to them, in addition to areas of inquires cited earlier for immigrants.

Family Life Cycle and Stages of Development

As with individuals, families go through a certain predictable life cycle: marriage, birth and raising of children, departure of children from home, retirement, and death. Family stress is often greatest at transition points from one stage to another of the family developmental process. Timing of transitions from one stage to the next and certain dynamics may vary for Asian American families because of socialization, child-rearing practices, and marital and parental role expectations. Nevertheless, family members' adjustment to demands and tasks imposed by different stages of the family life cycle remain constant. These adjustments and demands require considerable effort and energy under the most ideal situation. With many Asian American immigrant and refugee families, the added stress of relocation, the search for economic security, the barriers of language and other cultural differences, development of a sense of new identity, and incorporation of new beliefs and values systems can be extremely overwhelming.

Migration may be more disruptive at a particular stage in the family life cycle, such as adolescence, by interfering with processes involving adjustment (e.g., establishing appropriate limits for adolescents; del Carman, 1990). All stages of development have their own demands, but adolescence can be especially difficult for parents and children in Asian American families. Normative struggles of separation and independence are compounded by other cultural issues, such as respect of elderly persons, strict discipline of children, and dating customs among the young. Conflicts escalate between Asian American parents and adolescents because of the different acculturation rate between the two generations discussed earlier. Many Asian American adolescents also suffer from internal identity conflicts due to their inability to reconcile vast differences between their culture of origin and the majority culture in the U.S. Parental attitudes toward their own ethnic identity and their level of comfort with being bicultural individuals, prior successful resolutions of parent–child conflicts, and availability of mediators from among extended family members or community are some of the areas for clinicians to explore to assess the extent of conflicts, capacity for change, and effective strategies for intervention.

Conclusion

Asian American families have special needs and present different clinical challenges to mental health professionals. Despite studies that indicate changing roles and family patterns among Asian American parents in the direction of greater similarity to European American values and practice, Asian ethnic values and norms continue to play an important role in family life for many generations (McGoldrick, 1982). One should not automatically assume a loss of traditional family values with increasing resident years in the United States. Other variables, such as family upbringing, geographical location (ethnic enclaves vs. fully integrated communities), and prior exposure to and immersion in Western culture, influence cultural identity and values. Clinical assessment is a process for gaining understanding to make appropriate and effective interventions. A multimodel approach is a systems approach that evaluates Asian American families. Variables considered here are seen as basic and relevant elements for a comprehensive and culturally competent assessment of these families. Circumstances vary and new knowledge emerges; family counselors need to maintain a flexible and responsive stance.

References

American Psychiatric Association. (1994). *Diagnostic and statistical manual of mental disorders* (4th ed.). Washington, DC: Author.

Arkoff, H., Meredith, G., & Doug, J. (1963). Attitudes of Japanese Americans and Caucasian Americans and Caucasian American students toward marriage roles. *Journal of Social Psychology, 59,* 11–15.

Chia, R. C., Chong, C. J., Cheng, B. S., Castlellow, W., Moore, W., & Hayes, M. (1985). Attitudes toward marriage roles among Chinese and American college students. *Journal of Social Psychology, 126,* 31–35.

Chin, J. L. (1983). Diagnosis considerations in working with Asian Americans. *American Journal of Orthopsychiatry, 53,* 100–109.

Congress, E. P. (1994). The use of culturagrams to assess and empower culturally diverse families. *Families in Society, 75,* 531–540.

del Carman, R. (1990). Assessment of Asian-Americans for family therapy. In F. C. Serafica, A. I. Schwebel, R. K. Russell, P. D. Issac, & L. B. Meyers (Eds.), *Mental health of ethnic minorities* (pp. 139–166) New York: Prager.

Garfield, S. L. (1983). Effectiveness of psychotherapy: The perennial controversy. *Professional Psychologist: Research and Practice, 14,* 35–43.

Ho, M. K.(1987). *Family therapy with ethnic minorities.* Newbury Park, CA: Sage.

Hsu, J., Tseng, W., Ashton, G., McDermott, J. F., & Char, W. (1985). Family interaction patterns among Japanese-American families and Caucasian families in Hawaii. *American Journal of Psychiatry, 142,* 577–581.

Johnson, J. H., Rasbury, W. C., & Siegel, L. J. (1986). *Approaches to child treatment.* New York: Pergamon Press.

Kazdin, A. E. (1988). *Child Psychotherapy: Developing and identifying effective treatments.* New York: Pergamon Press.

Lee, E. (1982). A social systems approach to assessment and treatment for Chinese American families. In M. McGoldrick, J. K. Pearce, and J. Giordana (Eds.), *Ethnicity and family therapy* (pp. 527–551). New York: Guilford Press.

Lee, E. (1996). Asian American families: An overview. In M. McGoldrick, J. Giordana, & J. K. Pearce (Eds.), *Ethnicity and family therapy* (2nd ed., pp. 227–248). New York: Guilford Press.

Lee, E. & Oberst, G. (1989). My mother's purpose dress. In Asian Women United of California, *Making waves.* Boston: Beacon Press.

Lum, D. (1995). *Social work practice and people of color* (3rd ed.). Pacific Grove, CA: Brooks/Cole.

McDermott, J. F., Char, W. F., Hsu, J., Tseng, W., & Ashton, G. (1983). Cultural variations and family attitudes and their implications for therapy. *Journal of the American Academy of Child Psychiatry, 22,* 454–458.

McGoldrick, M. (1982). *Ethnicity and family therapy: An overview.* In M. McGoldrick, J. K. Pearce, & J. K. Giordana (Eds.), *Ethnicity and family therapy* (pp. 3–30). New York: Guilford Press.

McGoldrick, M., & Giordana, J. (1996). An overview: Ethnicity and family therapy. In M. McGoldrick, J. Giordana, & J. K. Pearce (Eds.), *Ethnicity and family therapy* (pp. 1–27). New York: Guilford Press.

Shon, S. P., & Ja, D. Y. (1982). Asian families. In M. McGoldrick, J. K. Pearce, & J. Giordana (Eds.), *Ethnicity and family therapy* (pp. 208–228). New York: Guilford Press.

Tran, T. V. (1993). Psychological traumas and depression in a sample of Vietnamese people in the United States. *Social Work, 18*, 184–194

Uba, L. (1994). *Asian Americans: Personality patterns, identity, and mental health.* New York: Guilford Press.

U.S. Department of Health and Human Services. (1993). *Report to Congress: Refugee Resettlement Program.* Washington, DC: U.S. Government Printing Office.

Weaver, D. R. (1982). Empowering treatment skills for helping Black families. *Social Casework, 63*, 100–105.

Wong, B. (1985). Family, kinship, and ethnic identity of the Chinese in New York City, with comparative remarks on the Chinese in Lima, Peru, and Manila, Philippines. *Journal of Comparative Family Studies, 16*, 231–252.

■ ■ ■

3

Understanding Cultural Values in Counseling Asian Families

Xiaolu Hu, PhD
Gong Chen, EdD

Culture is a complex social phenomenon. Anthropologists have managed to collect over a million cultural elements for scientists to study (Laudin, 1973). Considerable debate and controversy continue to rage over an accurate description of how one learns about a culture and what is needed to learn about a culture. Therefore, counselors often feel overwhelmed by the tasks of understanding different cultures and knowing how to work with clients or families from a culture different from their own. To foster counselors' multicultural competence, this chapter addresses the importance of understanding cultural values when counseling Asian families and how value systems are related to family issues.

The Importance of Understanding Asian Cultural Values

To address cultural values while counseling Asian clients, it is essential to reach a definition of culture. Although considerable debate and controversy continue to rage over an accurate definition (Banks, 1987), culture has been variously defined as the following:

1. A broad meaning that includes a full range of social system variables, such as demographic factors (age, sex, and place of residence), and status variables, such as social, educational, and economic levels.
2. A narrowly defined concept limited to ethnographic variables, such as nationality and ethnicity, although it may include language and religion.

According to Laudin (1973), all cultures have certain basic common traits; however, cultures are not the same in form.

Researchers have also generally defined and studied culture from many different perspectives. To understand the impact of culture on human behavior, Laudin (1973) identified five levels of influential elements of culture. He asserted that the first level of culture is a foundation of factors that begin with biology and, by extension or implication, includes psychology. The second level is ideology, consisting of values and beliefs that are characteristic of individuals. The third level is cultural attitude. These are conscious or unconscious processes that either precede or follow certain behaviors and are constantly fed by values and beliefs. Once it has been formed, it is often very difficult to change an attitude, and it would be more difficult to change an attitude in an older person than in a child. The fourth level of culture is behavior, which is related to attitudes, ideologies, values, and beliefs. The fifth level of culture is the social situation variable. On the basis of this description, the five variables are all interrelated in a dynamic structure. Among them, the second level, ideology, seems to be a crucial element that creates a pattern of dynamic behavior. Ideology consists of values and beliefs, and it influences a total culture.

Many researchers have studied culture on the basis of their own professional interests. For example, anthropologists (Laudin, 1973) are primarily concerned with acculturation and the nature of social processes; educators try to improve the performance of minority students by increasing the congruence between the school and various cultures (Baruth & Manning, 1992); and sociologists study the interaction of cultures and social–economic advancement. To improve the quality of counseling services to ethnic and culturally diverse populations, counseling professionals are more interested in the culture within the person (Pedersen, 1994)—how external elements, ethnographic, social, educational, economic, and demographic variables make an impact on people's beliefs, values, behavior, ideas, and personalities. Significant literature has contributed to understanding human beliefs, personality, ideology, and behavior, but little significant literature has provided a systematic knowledge of cultural values. Value is an abstract principle concerning the patterns of behavior within a particular culture or society that, through the process of socialization, the members of that society hold in high regard.

Cultural values are crucial elements of a culture that control and influence a person's dynamic behavior. Cultural values, called social values, form central principles around which individual and societal goals can be integrated. Classic examples of American cultural values include freedom, justice, education, and privacy. Typical Asian cultural values include harmony, family, social order, and education.

It is essential to understand Asian cultural values and how they influence the counseling process. Seeking to understand Asian values can be a stepping-stone in allowing counselors to foster a systematic knowledge, as well as insights, of a culture. Sue, Ivey, and Pedersen (1996) stressed, "Culturally learned patterns provide orderly and systematic narratives in which each part of the client's identity relates dynamically to the whole" (p. 18). Without a knowledge of these values, misunderstandings can occur in diagnosis and therapy. For example, Asian clients may smile through a counseling session to be polite and to show respect to the counselor. If the counselor lacks an understanding of the cultural value system, that nonverbal language could be interpreted as an establishment of good rapport in counseling or that clients may not be seriously depressed or concerned about their problems.

It is critical to understand cultural values when working with families that have diverse cultural backgrounds, just as Sue, et al. (1996) stressed that "culturally learned patterns do provide an orderly and systematic narratives in which each part of the client's identity relates dynamically to the whole" (p. 18). Unfortunately, as mental health professionals, we have not paid enough attention to cultural values to reach a systematic knowledge about values systems in different cultures.

Asian Cultural Values Versus American Cultural Values

Certain aspects of Asian cultural values conflict with American cultural values (see Table 1). Huang (1995) stated that "Americans tend to focus on the individual, whereas Asians tend to focus on the family that the individual comes from. American culture provides a greater degree of individuality and independence. Asian cultures frown on individuality and tend to promote family interdependence" (pp. 130–131). This difference results in opposite sets of behavior. It can also result in confusion, frustration, and value conflict.

First, the cultural value conflict can occur as a generation gap in the family. First-generation immigrants often identify with the culture in which they grew up and expect their children to maintain the same culture and traditions. The second American-born generation is socialized with the culture their parents came from and with dominant American culture. They may experience more difficulty in determining how they should act and behave.

Second, cultural value conflict can occur as a very different behavior pattern in a social contact. For example, Asian American and dominant American culture may hold different sets of values about career development. The differences can be found in career choice, job performance, collegial relationships, and employer–employee relationships. Mainstream American culture highly values self-confidence, assertiveness, and communication skills. These are always perceived as successful characteristics of political leaders, administrators, and business managers (Callana & Greenhaus, 1990). The majority of Asian Americans have been perceived as quiet and introverted by Americans. More specifically, Asian women tend to be viewed as passive and submissive, and Asian men are seen as nonassertive and nonmasculine.

Studying Asian value systems proves that Asian culture places a strong emphasis on the behaviors or mannerisms of humbleness, harmony, and modesty (Hu & Chen, 1993). Asians believe that they always have lessons to learn and can always improve themselves. It is shameful for an individual to feel good about him- or herself; that is interpreted as showing disrespect to others. Self-satisfaction is seen in Asian culture as a sign of selfishness or a lack of making progress. Under the influence of these values, Asians tend to be more reserved. Even extroverted Asians perhaps are not viewed as being as expressive as their mainstream counterparts (Hu & Chen, 1993). These different value systems guide culturally diverse people to perform and behave differently. The different behavior and patterns are often misunderstood and misinterpreted. This is one of the major reasons for Asian Americans' overwhelming feeling that their strengths are not being valued, that they have reached a (possibly a self-imposed or perceived) glass ceiling, or that they are being discriminated against.

Fundamental Asian Cultural Values

Wenhao, Salomon, and Chay (1999) asserted that Asians hold a unique cultural value system. Their values are profoundly rooted in mind and habit. As in Europe or other continents, Asia contains distinct countries with a diversity of languages, religions, significant regional subcultures, and different political systems and social economic classes. Nevertheless, Asian cultural heritage and background may still lead them to share significant similarities in values. Some major values related to Asian families are discussed here.

Family Values

In the long history of civilization in Asian countries, although governments have come and gone, families have remained. Thus, the family has been the strongest social unit to provide guidance, support, and help to individuals. Because of this, it is important to keep the family name, a close family relationship, and family honor and to improve the family's social status. Each one of these family values guides Asians to perform in a particular way in society.

To carry a family's name, it becomes critical for Asians to become married and to have children, especially sons. Family members who have not married after they reach age 30 or 40, or who are not involved in a heterosexual relationship would not only feel more pressure and anxiety about marriage or sexual issues but also might experience a great deal of tension at home and amongst their relatives, especially their elders. Because sons carry the family's surname, a burdensome issue for families is pressure to have sons.

To maintain a close family relationship, everyone in the family must take responsibility for the care of family members, sometimes sacrificing self to help the family. Children feel obligated to help their elder parent. Moving away or living too far away to care for elderly parents or relatives can make these family members feel quite guilty. If there is an ill parent in the family, the children, especially the oldest, has the responsibility to care for that parent, even if it means abandoning the new American lifestyle and returning to the old country.

To keep the family's honor—as Sue (1981) called family welfare and integrity—everyone in the family has a responsibility to make the family proud. Failures in school, business, or marriage; bad luck; mistakes; or misbehavior are all considered an embarrassment, shame, and loss of face to the entire family. None can be tolerated. Therefore, for many families, it is difficult to discuss problems with outsiders, even confidential professionals. If a family knows an independent counselor who understands the client's culture, however, talking to the counselor about their secret problems may be a better choice to these Asians than talking to their friends. This way they do not have to feel a loss of face or a loss of family honor.

Commitment to family is internalized for Asians. Traditionally, it may be normal or customary among Asian families never to express thanks, appreciation, or love to one another verbally. As Yagi and Oh (1995) described, Asian children "grow up never hearing the actual words *I love you* from their parents" (p. 70). It is very rare to see Asian family members arguing or hugging and kissing each other in public, especially in the presence of members of the family's perceived community. It does not necessarily mean that children or family members feel a lack of love. Love and appreciation are simply expressed differently. Very often, one's love and affection are expressed through a devotion to the family. Many Asian parents may give up their career or lifestyle, sometimes working long hours to ensure a good education and a promising future for their children (Yagi & Oh, 1995). In turn, children are expected to perform well and be successful to make their parents proud. To them, this is a much deeper level of love.

Harmony and Modesty

As a fundamental belief, Chinese "yin and yang" philosophy has been well taken in American society. Another key concept, has had a continuing role in Chinese history for more than 2,000 years: "Ren," or benevolence, which has rarely been explored by American researchers. Ren is a central notion of Confucian ideology that has had critical influence in Chinese and many other Asian cultures and histories. It served as a basic principle to maintain peace, harmony, and social order in ancient China. Benevolence does not just mean kindness. It also means loyalty, to sacrifice oneself for the benefit of others in higher authority. To achieve social order and harmony, most Asian cultures regulated the social order by establishing a rigid hierarchical authority. This system demands obedience from all subjects. For example, if the father is absent, the oldest son will be in charge. Therefore, being humble, being modest, and showing respect to other people became important values in Asian society. Sue (1981) noted that in Chinese culture "ancestors and elders are viewed with great reverence and respect.

The roles of family members are rigidly defined, allowing for few significant deviations. Conflicts within the family are minimized, because the structure is so arranged that roles do not interfere with others.... Much effort is expended to avoid offending others" (p. 121).

This history influences many Asian value systems, including respect for authorities, respect for parents, loyalty, and a sacrifice of individual needs for the benefit of society or family. Parsons (1966) called it collectivism. Huang (1995) called it group oriented and group dependent. Because of this tradition of Ren, Asians may tend to be more interdependent, collective, flexible, and conventional.

Friendship has traditionally been a factor of harmony to many Asian Americans. For friends, Asians are willing to sacrifice everything. Especially in America, where many Asian Americans are isolated in their own cultural and language circles, friendship plays a very important role for them to survive and achieve in the dominant culture. For many Asians, friendship can be a great resource for seeking help, support, information, and guidance.

Education

Asian Americans are known for their value of education. Yagi and Oh (1995) stated that "educational achievement is paramount for people and academic success is related to family honor. Because of this, young people often have great academic expectations imposed on them by parents " (pp. 64–65). It is believed that education is an essential means to success and improvement in the quality of life, a result of a long history. Traditionally, in most Asian countries, education was the only way to change family status. There has been more than 2,000 years of history of official government examination systems in China. Once one passed an exam, no matter how poor or rich, he could become a royal official overnight. In contemporary society, education is continued to be seen as having the greatest value for an Asian American's success in the mainstream culture. Because of socialization to this traditional value, significant numbers of Asian families can successfully motivate their children to aspire to high status and educational achievement. Of course, not all Asian Americans fit into so-called "model minority" myths. Those who have to struggle with their education have more pressure from their family and society. They not only have to face the challenges of intensive study but also the expectations of their family and social bias of the common perception of the Asian American "model student."

It is often said that Asians are more likely to turn to their family for advice, and Asian students are more likely to choose college majors based on their parents' expectations. It was found that Asian parents often place pressure on their children to obtain more education rather than provide their children with specific direction in choosing a college major (Hu, 1992).

Industry

Although Asian cultures value education, historically, only a limited number of people could afford it. For most people, the only way to improve family status has been through hard work and saving money. In most Asian countries, life has improved slowly during the past few centuries. To improve a family's social status, all members of the family must work hard toward this goal. This may be one of the reasons many Asian Americans choose their careers on the basis of status and salary rather than vocational interests. To be successful in society, Asian Americans expect their children to follow the footsteps of Asians who have previously made their way successfully. Very often, these role models are doctors, engineers, scientific researchers, lawyers, and other "honorable" professionals.

Working hard has always meant working long hours, keeping busy, and often sacrificing personal life or family time. Unlike American culture, creativity is seen as an important personal feature, but not one for the workplace. Many Asian professionals are proud of how busy they are, their business indicating or implying that they work hard and contribute to the family honor.

Caveat

Although this discussion has itself made generalizations regarding typical Asian cultural values, it should be noted that there are differing values amongst different Asian groups. Even among Chinese people, there are differing value systems between, for example, recent immigrants from the mainland and multigeneration immigrants from Canton who immigrated through Hong Kong. Mainland Chinese immigrants, brought up under Communist rule with little religion- or tradition-based lifestyles, have generally crossed halfway around the world, leaving their parents and extended families behind. Cantonese immigrants have generally retained very close family ties with high levels of ancient family tradition that are still practiced, at least for a few generations, in the United States. The latter may even be perceived as rigid in Western eyes, and the former is somewhat closer to American mainstream values.

One difficulty for counselors may be distinguishing among the different Asian groups. Despite this, the counselor must educate him- or herself to recognize cultural value differences between particular clients and mainstream culture. Without a knowledge of the underlying beliefs and values of clients, the counselor will lack effectiveness in counseling.

The study of cultural value systems can provide a different way of learning about clients in a counseling relationship. Very few studies in multicultural counseling have systematically analyzed various cultural values. Most research has addressed only a few issues relating to different customs, traditions, lifestyles, personal contact patterns, and religions. If one can obtain an understanding of the role cultural values play in minority populations, a different point of view toward the personality of these groups of people may be obtained.

Conclusion

In view of the foregoing, the degree of the counselor's culture sensitivity is directly related to his or her knowledge of multicultural differences. Learning minority value systems may result in a better and more positive understanding of minority populations. It also may help to recognize cultural differences as strengths that are valuable and enriching to personal growth and to the counseling process, as well as the counseling relationship. As Isaacson and Brown (1993) stated, understanding cultural differences, especially the factor of values, and adjusting one's approach appropriately may be the secret to successful counseling with multicultural clients.

Although various factors play important roles affecting counseling Asian families, cultural values are an underresearched component of counseling. To a certain extent, traditional Asian American cultural beliefs conflict with values inherent in dominant American culture. The amount of conflict varies with the level of cultural assimilation. It may be hypothesized that people who adopt mainstream culture or hold similar values to the mainstream culture face less value conflict than people who have not assimilated with that culture. The counselor must be prepared to gauge the presence and amount of cultural conflict or assimilation.

TABLE 1
Common Cultural Value Differences and Conflicts

U.S. Dominant Culture	Conflicting Values of Asian Cultures
Self-fulfillment and self-actualization	Family welfare and well-being
Self-esteem	Other-esteem (Huang, 1995) and respect for elders and ancestors
Love and affection	Internalized love and action to show love
Independence and self-efficiency	Interdependence and filial duty
Assertiveness and confidence	Humility and harmony
Creativity	Hard work and industry
Verbal communication	Action as a higher priority than effective speaking skills
Expression of emotions	Control over emotions
Individual privacy	Family privacy
Community involvement	Deep friendship with a few and willingness to die for friends
Change and fast past	Patience and tolerance
Happiness	Success
Saving of time, time is money	Frugality, saving of money

References

Banks, J. A. (1987). *Teaching strategies for ethnic studies* (4th ed.). Boston: Allyn & Bacon.

Baruth, L., & Manning, M. L. (1992). *Multicultural education of children and adolescents.* Needham Heights, MA: Allyn & Bacon.

Callana, G. A., & Greenhaus, J. H. (1990). The career indecision of managers and professionals: Development of a scale and test of a model. *Journal of Vocational Behavior, 37,* 79–103.

Hu, X. (1992, November). *Career development of Asian women.* Paper presented at the California Career Conference, Oakland, CA.

Hu, X., & Chen, G. (1993, December). *Understanding cultural values in counseling Asian clients.* Paper presented at the International Counseling Conference, Vancouver, British Columbia, Canada.

Huang, P. O. (1995). *Other-esteem—A creative response to a society obssessed with promoting the self.* San Diego, CA: Black Rorrest Press.

Isaacson, L. E., & Brown, D. (1993). *Career information, career counseling, & career development.* Needham Heights, MA: Allyn & Bacon.

Laudin, H. (1973). *Victims of culture.* Columbus, OH: Charles E. Merrill.

Parsons, T. (1966). *The social system.* Toronto, Ontario, Canada: Collier-Macmillan.

Pedersen, P. (1994). *A handbook for developing multicultural awareness.* Alexandria, VA: American Counseling Association.

Sue, D. W. (1981). *Counseling the culturally different: Theory and practice.* New York: Wiley.

Sue, D. W., Ivey, A. E., & Pedersen, P. B. (1996). *A theory of multicultural counseling and therapy.* Pacific Grove, CA: Brooks/Cole.

Wenhao, J., Salomon, H. B., & Chay, D. M. (1999). Transcultural counseling and people of Asian origin: A developmental and therapeutic perspective. In J. McFadden (Ed.), *Transcultural counseling* (2nd ed. p. 261). Alexandria, VA: American Counseling Association.

Yagi, D. T., & Oh, M. Y. (1995). Counseling Asian American students. In C. C. Lee (Ed.), *Counseling for diversity: A guide for school counselors and related professionals* (p. 70). Needham Heights, MA: Allyn & Bacon.

■■■

PART

COUNSELING
ASIAN FAMILIES

4

Counseling Chinese Families: A Postmodern Approach

Shi-Juian Wu, PhD

Counseling Chinese Families: A Postmodern Approach

The postmodern approach to family therapy has been applied mostly to the mainstream population since its development less than 2 decades ago. There have been minimal research and clinical application of this approach with Chinese families. Anderson and Goolishian (1992) have advocated that a postmodern approach can enable therapists to categorize different families, different therapists, and different therapies. This concept has yet to be tested with the Chinese population. This chapter introduces and explores how a postmodern approach can be applied to the Chinese population at different levels.

Postmodernism

Postmodern inquiry is another way of constructing one's reality and perception of the world that we live in. Its tenets are not based on seeking ultimate truths and absolute knowledge, but on the processes by which people come to describe, explain, or account for the world in which they live (Gergen, 1985). It emphasizes depathologizing, holding a nonexpert stance, having curiosity, searching for untold stories, generating meaning, and collaborating. It helps people to revisit their life by retelling their stories and identifying their resources through narratives.

Postmodernism distinguishes the person from the problem. The problem is no longer equated with self-identity. Postmodernism also redefines beliefs normally accepted through observation and examination (Gergen, 1985). The aim of postmodernism is to have less focus on facts and open other possibilities of meanings and understandings. Because clients' knowledge is more privileged than the professional's (Friedman, 1995), the clinician is no longer the expert, which shifts the hierarchical nature of therapy and allows clients to be viewed as the experts. This idea should not be confused with the idea that the clinician does not know or do anything. The clinician is like an expert in orchestrating a symphony, but clients are the musicians who create the music.

As the clinician moves away from being the expert, he or she becomes very curious about what clients have to disclose and less interested in preconceived understanding, analysis, and explanation of the presenting problem. This intersubjective notion of cocreating meaning through collaborative conversation is what hermeneutics is based on (Anderson & Goolishian, 1992). Curiosity is always reflected on looking for not-yet-told stories, and the clinician cointerprets these narratives with clients. This collaborative, therapeutic conversation becomes a generative process of creating new meanings that can be useful for clients.

Anderson and Goolishian (1988) described the human system as a linguistic system and wrote that the human system is not the problem, but conversing about problems tends to enhance the human system. Communication and discourse define social organization, rather than social organization defining communication and discourse. As conversation moves along, problems become more evident. This is very different from the traditional family therapy approaches, which often view and label the family as dysfunctional.

Postmodern Development in Family Therapy

One of the first postmodern family therapy groups was pioneered by Harry Goolishian and Harleen Anderson from Galveston, Texas, in the 1980s. They believed that therapy is a collaborative language system and placed central emphasis on the role of language and dialogue in the social construction of meaning (Anderson & Goolishian, 1992). The therapist takes a "not-knowing" position with genuine interest and curiosity, wanting to understand the client's reality. He or she expresses a need to know more about what has just been said, rather than conveying preconceived understandings about what needs to be changed.

Another group, led by Tom Andersen, had clinicians reflect on how therapy was done with different families. This has been known as the "reflecting team" approach (Andersen, 1991), which allows professionals to observe behind a one-way mirror and eventually present their intervention ideas to the family members. As Bateson stated, "Difference makes differences" (Keeney, 1983) when families hear different voices expressing differing views because a new level of understanding could emerge. Families are also invited to share their experiences with the reflecting team.

Lynn Hoffman (1993) has been very much influenced by Tom Andersen's concept of "reflexive conversation." This process is mutually influenced by the clinician and clients, creating a sense of equality rather than hierarchy. She has also used the concept of the reflecting team and reflecting conversation and addressed the concern of how the mental health field has colonized people who seek help. She has encouraged professionals not to repeat that colonization process.

Many more ideas borrowed from the basic concept of the reflecting team also emerged (Friedman, 1995). One such example is to invite the community as audience and witness for clients (Lobovits, Maisel, & Freeman, 1995); circulating clients' successful archives with other clients who go through similar problems (Madigan & Epston, 1995); and having people who have overcome a particular life problem act as social advocate for their peers, particularly among adolescents with very difficult problems (Madigan & Epston, 1995). Among the narrative approach proponents, Michael White from Australia and David Epston from New Zealand are the most influential individuals. White (1992) favored postmodernism more than essentialism, which searches for absolute truths and true knowledge. He has written that people tend to internalize their problems with the result that their self-identity becomes inseparable from the reality of the problem. He has used deconstruction of knowledge and externalization theory to help people reauthorize their lives through identifying unique outcomes.

Another model that has attracted a large group of practitioners is the brief solution-focused therapy developed by Berg and de Shazer. They have stated that clients do not need to talk about the history of their problem to solve the problem. In reality, problem talk can perpetuate the cycle or cause clients to repeat the problem, so they have advocated shifting from problem talk into solution talk. Whenever a problem is addressed, the counselor should help the person to identify and focus on the solutions underlying the problem.

Application of Postmodern Theory to Chinese Families

Before we explore the idea of applying postmodern theory to Chinese families, we need to clarify what we mean by Chinese families. Chinese Americans have grown in number since the 1980s, from 806,040 in 1980 to 1,645,472 in 1990 (Fong, 1992). Among them, 63% of Chinese Americans were foreign born in 1984 compared with only 39% in 1965 (Takaki, 1989). This trend continues to grow. Special attention must be given to the growing number of foreign-born Chinese individuals and their families. Chinese families are very diverse in terms of their country of origin, dialects, cultural values, and degrees of acculturation.

According to Wu (1994), Keeney (1983), and Moore (1978), family therapy literature tends to reduce Chinese families into categories and "inanimate monoliths" rather than describe their complex cultural experiences. The traditional approach named clinicians as experts who provide treatment and structure on how Chinese families should interact. It is important to understand that Chinese families do not belong to only one category. The postmodern approach allows Chinese families to explore the marginalized part of their stories, to use their own community resources, and to begin to claim their self-identity as experts instead of letting professionals define what their stories are supposed to be.

The following section is a case example using the key concepts of the postmodern approach in working with Chinese families.

Case Example

Fe Fe is a 6-year-old first-grade Chinese girl studying at an elementary school in the United States. She came with her mother, a 35-year-old Mandarin-speaking Chinese woman from China slightly more than a year ago, to join their father. Two months ago, a dog bit Fe Fe on her right hand while she was walking with her mother in their neighborhood. Since then, Fe Fe has been terrified by the sight of a dog and becomes panicky whenever she sees a dog. She runs, screams, and becomes out of control even when her mother is with her. She has also experienced frequent nightmares and crying spells in the middle of night. Her teacher raised concerns to Fe Fe's mother about her concentration at school. Her mother at first could not connect Fe Fe's symptom and the dog bite, and she eventually decided to seek therapy for her daughter.

Fe Fe was in therapy for a total of eight sessions. A summary of each session, as well as the core excerpts from the therapy conversation, is presented. Theoretical applications and cultural issues are discussed at the end of each excerpt.

First Session. According her mother, Fe Fe used to love dogs, but since she was attacked by a dog 2 months ago, she screamed whenever she saw any dog. Another concern the mother (M) had was that Fe Fe (FF) was unable to concentrate on her school work and had frequent nightmares. The clinician (C) wanted to find out from the mother what she expected from therapy.

C: Knowing that you have concerns for your daughter, what would you like to see happen in the sessions? (She invites the mother to define the treatment focus. This is to set up a collaborative tone.)

M: I'd like my daughter not to be afraid of dogs and be able to concentrate on her studies. But I don't know how to help her and I hope you can help her. (The mother is clear about what she wants from her point of view and wants the clinician to accomplish the goals).

C: It's normal for Fe Fe to respond to dogs the way she has been because she was traumatized by the incident. It was something unexpected and she did not prepare herself to face the situation. The experience put her in a position of feeling unable to do anything. If she knows what she could do whenever she sees a dog, it might help decrease her anxiety. Does this explanation make sense to you? (The clinician is paying attention to the mother's language on having the clinician to be the expert to help her daughter. At the same time, the clinician is planning to help the mother to become the expert as well. At Fe Fe's developmental age, she probably will not be able to express what happened to her internally. The clinician sympathizes with the mother's general reaction toward the trauma.)

M: It makes sense that that's why she is panicky. So what can we do at this moment? (The mother was invited to comment on the clinician's overall factual understanding and was invited to provide input.)

C: What I will do is to understand Fe Fe's fear with your help. Let her express her fear and anger and explore ways to deal with dogs so that she will feel more in control. Would that be okay for you? (It's important to inform the mother of the possible treatment plan and expected treatment outcomes; therefore, treatment becomes a collaborative endeavor between the clinician and the family. The words *with your help* invite the mother to be the expert in helping her daughter. The clinician also asked whether the treatment was okay to get her collaboration.)

M: Yes! I want to give it a try.

The clinician (C) decided to approach Fe Fe (FF).

C: Your mother has told me about your experience with a dog; can you also tell me what happened? (Fe Fe sits next to her mother.)

FF: I was walking down the street, and all of a sudden a dog came out and grabbed my hand. (The mother looks at and listens to her.)

C: How were you feeling then?

FF: I was very scared.

C: Of course. I would be scared, too. Was your mom with you? (Her mother can be part of Fe Fe's resource in dealing with her safety.)

FF: Yes! I held my mom's hand very tightly. My mom saw the dog and yelled at it and the dog eventually left me alone. (Her mother is a symbol of safety for Fe Fe. The goal is to help Fe Fe to create safety for herself.)

C: It was good that your mom was with you and you held her hand tightly, so that she could help you. (This helps Fe Fe understand that at least her mother was there; however, eventually the therapy plan is for her to learn to be in control of the situation.)

C: Continue holding your mother's hand since it seems to help you. (Because Fe Fe is still fearful of facing dogs, it is not appropriate to send her away without any recommendation. This recommendation also implies that Fe Fe has done her best to protect herself and that she has done nothing wrong. She needs to continue doing whatever works.)

Although Fe Fe was the one who experienced the problem, her mother was invited into the session to work with the clinician and help her daughter by gradually becoming the cotherapist. At the end, the mother appreciated the new understanding about the possible emotional impact on her daughter as dramatized by the dog and wanted to work with the clinician in trying different ways to help Fe Fe. During the session, the mother did not say much, but she was invited to comment on what the clinician was doing.

Lee (1989) stated that Chinese families prefer to view the therapist as the problem solver, not as a peer. In this case, however, the clinician slowly coached the mother to become her daughter's expert and helper. The clinician can be the expert who helps the mother become her own expert at assisting her child. Therapy becomes more time effective when the client's goals are given priority (Friedman, 1995). Helping families to set up measurable short-term goals is vital (Lee, 1989), but paying attention to the cultural aspect of preferred goals is rarely discussed in research literature. In this case example, the mother talked about her daughter's not being able to concentrate on her study. For most Chinese parents, their children's ability to do well in school is critical. Another aspect of the preferred outcome is for Fe Fe not to fear any dog. In Chinese culture, teaching children to be strong and self-disciplined is very significant. When Fe Fe is no longer afraid of a dog, she can be strong again and deal with many hardships in her life.

Not involving Fe Fe's father in the session is debatable. According to her mother, she is the one who raises her daughter and feels she can handle the situation without burdening her husband, who is a very busy graduate student and also works part time. From most traditional systems approaches, the father may be included in the session; however, from this culture standpoint, not involving the father seems to be a respectful way to deal with the presenting problem.

Second Session. A week later, Fe Fe's mother came with her again and stated that Fe Fe basically remained the same. Fe Fe still had nightmares and could not concentrate on her school work. A few days before, Fe Fe went with her mother and a friend to a beach close to their home where they saw two dogs. The clinician asked Fe Fe what she did when she saw the dogs. Fe Fe responded that she held her mother's hand tightly and did not look at the dogs. It was helping her to do that. The clinician congratulated her for doing such a good job in making herself safe and protected. She smiled, and her mother also followed the lead, telling her daughter that it was good to be able to hold her hand. The clinician asked the mother whether it was okay to help Fe Fe release her angry feeling toward the dog in a role-playing situation. The mother gave permission.

C: (Talking to Fe Fe) What does the dog look like? Can you draw it for me so I know what the dog looks like?

FF: Let me see.

C: Take your time.

FF: (Draws the dog. She also asks her mother some questions about the dog. The mother was coached to participate with her daughter as a way to show support to her.)

C: Are you angry at the dog?

FF: Yes!

C: What would you like to do to the dog?

FF: I want to lock the dog in jail.

C: Good idea! (There are many building blocks in the therapy room. The clinician suggests using them to build a jail.) Why don't we build a jail for the dog so you can lock the dog in and the dog won't come out to bite people. (The mother looks puzzled, and the clinician explains briefly to the mother how toys might be helpful to work with younger kids.)

FF: *Yes! I want to do that.* (The mother is again encouraged to help her daughter build the jail. At this point, the mother participates as much as she can in helping her daughter. The clinician is gently transferring the helping role to the mother.)

C: So what do you want to do now?

FF: I want to use a lock to lock the dog.

C: (They use another block to symbolize a lock on the jail.) The dog should not have bitten you; you did not do anything bad to the dog. The dog is not a good dog. What would you like to do about the dog?

FF: I want to tear up the dog (looking at the picture she drew).

C: I have a pair of scissors, do you want to use the scissors? (Asks the mother whether it is acceptable for Fe Fe to use the pair of scissors.)

FF: Yes! (By now, she can not wait to use the scissors. The mother helps Fe Fe cut the drawing into pieces.)

C: Are you angry at the dog for what it did to you?

FF: Yes! I want to kill the dog.

C: (Invites FF to choose a block to represent the dog)

FF: (Begins to use a pen to hit the "dog.")

C: (Invites the mother to join her daughter in releasing the anger. By now, the clinician, Fe Fe, and the mother are using different things to strike the wooden block.)

Before the clinician suggested the treatment for releasing Fe Fe's anger, she reviewed and discussed with the mother how children might respond when something shocking happened and that it might be helpful to release that angry feeling in a symbolic way. Fe Fe's mother, because of her cultural background, was unaware of how to deal with that type of anger. The clinician decided to provide the information before any treatment decision was made, and the mother agreed to try this approach to help Fe Fe.

Third Session. Fe Fe and her mom went to the beach again the following week. They saw the same dogs, but her mother told Fe Fe not to be afraid. Fe Fe was less fearful and was able to manage herself better without screaming. She chose not to look at the dog and held her mother's hand tightly. According to her mom, Fe Fe still was affected by the sight of a dog. She had fewer nightmares and seemed to have other dreams, which she termed "funny dreams." At this moment, her best strategy, according to Fe Fe, in dealing with her fear was not to look at a dog. The clinician wanted to check with Fe Fe and assess how she could make sense of her funny dreams.

C: (Talking to Fe Fe) I'd like to know about your funny dreams. Can you draw for me what you dreamt a few days ago? (Drawing helps Fe Fe focus less on the threatening dreams and more on her funny dreams.)
FF: Yes! (She giggles as she draws. Her mother asks her to draw for the clinician.)
C: Can you tell me what you just drew?
FF: I dreamt that I did not wear my top to school.
C: How was that for you?
FF: It was funny.
C: So your dream is a little different now. You used to have some nightmares, but now you are having funny dreams. How is that for you?
FF: When I am dreaming funny dreams, I am not scared. (Retelling her story allows Fe Fe to know that she can experience fewer scary dreams and has a sense of safety.)
M: I guess you are right. I went to her bed less frequently to comfort her in the middle of night. I worry less whether she will have nightmares or not. (This is to create a mutual understanding between Fe Fe and her mom.)

Overall, at this point, Fe Fe was doing better with her mom's support and assurance. She learned to accept her anger toward the dog that bit her and also knew she could look to her mother for support. She did not have to scream or run away from dogs anymore. By developing such coping strategies, it is hoped that Fe Fe felt more in control and began to learn to differentiate between the dog that bit her and dogs who would not bite her. She began to increase her concentration on her studies, which is how the mother evaluated treatment effectiveness.

Fourth Session. Fe Fe dreamt several dreams related to swimming and monsters. Fe Fe was asked to draw how she got away from the monsters and she drew how she hid from the monsters. She thought the monsters were stupid and she knew how to trick them. A sense of pride was introduced in the session. The mother learned that her daughter's way of dealing with the monsters might be a reflection of how Fe Fe could regain her sense of control. The mother was invited to think about how she could continue to create an environment to allow Fe Fe to feel safer. Besides getting help from therapy, Fe Fe seemed to be able to identify different resources to help herself. Her mother still worried about Fe Fe's concentration problem, so the clinician decided to ask Fe Fe what she was thinking in the classroom before and after the dog attacked her.

C: (Talking to Fe Fe) I would like you to draw two pictures for me—one of what you were thinking in the classroom after the dog bit you, and one of what you think now when the teacher is talking to the students? (Fe Fe slowly draws two pictures with her mother's help.)
C: So tell me what is in the first picture.
FF: I think about the dog biting me. (The picture allows Fe Fe to share her experiences in a visual way.)
C: So it's hard for you to concentrate. How about the second picture?
FF: I thought about nothing. I just listened to the teacher.
C: So your mind followed the teacher's talking and you concentrated much better.
FF: Yes!

The goal for this interview was to examine where Fe Fe was in her level of concentration and to develop different strategies to cope with her problems. The goal of counseling was to make Fe Fe comfortable dealing with dogs, which would, it was hoped, help her to regain her full concentration. Her mother also emphasized how Fe Fe had stopped running away when she saw a dog. A role play was again suggested so that Fe Fe could demonstrate and practice what she and mother might do to help her further.

C: So, Fe Fe, you used to run away from dogs because you were scared. That was perfectly okay because you need to protect yourself. And your mom said you don't anymore. Here is a stuffed dog. Pretend that the dog is watching and may chase you. (The clinician holds the dog and pretends that it is going to chase Fe Fe.) Can you show me what you do when you see a dog? (Fe Fe is a bit scared, but she manages to show the clinician what she could do. Role-playing helps the scene become more vivid.)

FF: I will not run; instead, I will hold my mom's hand. (Her mother stood beside Fe Fe and gave her hand to her. Fe Fe smiles at her mom.)

C: How do you feel when you do that?

FF: I feel safer.

C: So you are doing something for yourself to feel safer. That's wonderful. Can you also show me what you would do when you see a dog? (Now the clinician holds the stuffed dog and pretends that it runs toward Fe Fe with her mother standing beside her. Fe Fe screams.)

C: So this was how you used to respond, but now you no longer need to run. Is that true? (This allows Fe Fe to have a sense of pride that she learned different strategies for coping with her fear of dogs.)

FF: Yes (smiling).

M: Fe Fe is much braver.

C: Definitely.

To involve her mother in the role play helped Fe Fe feel supported and allowed them to have some fun together. The indirect purpose of involving her mother was to coach her regarding different parenting styles and communication with Fe Fe. The mother expressed that she would use what she learned from the sessions at home to help her daughter. The clinician reviewed with Fe Fe's mother some of the useful strategies and congratulated her for doing such a good job.

Fifth Session. After 2 weeks, Fe Fe's mother disclosed that she had been doing much better. Fe Fe was able to recite ancient Chinese poems from the Tan Dynasty for as long as 30 min., which was a significant improvement in concentration. Fe Fe seemed to be less affected by dogs. In this session, she identified her personal experiences in addition to her mother's description.

C: Fe Fe, can you draw what you think when you recite poems?

FF: I think about words when I recite poems.

C: So thinking about words instead of dogs has helped you recite poems.

FF: Yes!

C: Can you also draw what you do when you see a dog? (Talking about Fe Fe's strategies in coping with her fear of dogs helps her to reinforce her experience of being able to take control and remember the strategies discussed from previous sessions.)

FF: (Drawing that she would not run) I will not run and will tell my mom that dogs are nasty.

C: That's quite a strategy!

It's interesting to note that Fe Fe's mother measured the success of her daughter by her ability to recite ancient poems. Many Chinese parents view reciting ancient poetry as the most critical learning experience for their children. Their belief is that reciting ancient poetry improves concentration, as well as the abilities of reading, writing, and knowledge. Different cultures may have different ways of measuring positive outcomes.

Sixth Session. Fe Fe continued holding hands with her mother when they came into the counselor's office. Her mother disclosed that Fe Fe saw a dog outside their home. She did panic; in fact, she expressed that that was a mean dog but that the stuffed dog was a cute dog. Fe Fe has clearly differentiated that not all dogs are mean.

Seventh Session. Fe Fe's mother disclosed that a few days before, Fe Fe saw a huge dog and told her that she was not intimidated by it while holding her hand tightly. She was even able to look at the dog and comment that the dog was big.

C: There are big and small dogs. How might you respond to them? (This assesses how Fe Fe responds to the different-sized dogs.)

FF: I am not afraid of small dogs, but I am afraid of big ones. (Fe Fe is learning about size of dogs and can respond to them differently).

C: That's a lot of progress. When you first came here, even a small dog was scary for you. Now you are not afraid of small dogs.

FF: Yes! The small ones do not scare me anymore.

C: Does your mom know that? Maybe you can tell her. (This is to help Fe Fe reclaim her success with family consensus and support.)

Eighth Session. Fe Fe was having fewer nightmares. In her dreams, she seemed to be able to fight back and experienced less anxiety. According to her mother, the school teacher felt that Fe Fe had begun to pay more attention in class, finish homework, and complete her writing on time. The clinician suggested termination because Fe Fe was doing much better. Her mother expressed that she was sad that the sessions were ending but felt confident that her daughter would continue to improve. Fe Fe was also congratulated for her accomplishment, and the clinician explained the process of termination. She was told that in the future, if things became difficult, she was welcome to come back. A follow-up was done 6 months later, and Fe Fe continued to do well at home and at school and expressed that she no longer feared dogs.

Conclusion

The approach described here generates a conversational context without pathologizing the problem. The treatment plan was always shared with her mother to gain her expertise and collaboration. In addition, her mother was able to provide pertinent information and serve as a resource for the child. The switch of context redefined the role of the clinician from being an expert to a conversationalist with the clients.

The clinician also helped the family develop different ways of dealing with anger in a culturally accepted way. This included educating the family on the impact of the child's trauma and explaining clearly how to express anger in a manageable way. It was also vital to accept Fe Fe's mother's authority and knowledge regarding her family situation. The clinician was mindful of the mother requesting an expert to provide the service, but gradually the authority was turned back to the mother. The nonexpert position, therefore, is applied in a culturally sensitive way. The counselor had to find out the mother's cultural definition of what it means to be effective in therapy. Regretfully, a child's voice is often neglected in family sessions. In this treatment, it is also equally critical to understand Fe Fe's detailed stories, coping strategies, and progress, along with her mother's support and how her mother witnessed Fe Fe's success.

References

Andersen, T. (1991). *The reflecting team: Dialogues and dialogues about the dialogues.* New York: Norton.

Anderson, H., & Goolishian, H. (1988). Human systems as linguistic systems: Evolving ideas about the implications for theory and practice. *Family Process, 27*, 371–393.

Anderson, H., & Goolishian, H. (1992). The client is the expert: A not-knowing approach to therapy. In S. McNamee & K. J. Gergen (Eds.), *Therapy as social construction* (pp. 25–39). Newbury Park, CA: Sage.

Fong, R. (1992). A history of Asian Americans. In S. M. Furuto, R. Biswas, D. K. Chung, K. M. Murase, & F. Ross-Sheriff (Eds.), *Social work practice with Asian Americans* (pp. 3–26). Newbury Park, CA: Sage.

Friedman, S. (1995). Closing reflections: On communities, connections, and conversations. In S. Friedman (Ed.), *The reflecting team in action: Collaborative practice in family therapy* (pp. 353–358). New York: Guilford Press.

Gergen, K. J. (1985). The social constructionist movement in modern psychology. *American Psychologist, 40*, 266–275.

Hoffman, L. (1993). *Exchanging voices: A collaborative approach to family therapy*. London: Karnac Boos.

Keeney, B. P. (1983). *Aesthetics of change*. New York: Guilford Press.

Lee, E. (1989). Assessment and treatment of Chinese-American immigrant families. *Journal of Psychotherapy and the Family, 6*, 99–122.

Lobovits, D., Maisel, R., & Freeman, J. C. (1995). Public practices: An ethic of circulation. In S. Friedman (Ed.), *The reflecting team in action: Collaborative practice in family therapy* (pp. 223–256). New York: Guilford Press.

Madigan, S., & Epston, D. (1995). From "spy-chiatric gaze" to communities of concern: From professional monologue to dialogue. In S. Friedman (Ed.), *The reflecting team in action: Collaborative practice in family therapy* (pp. 257–276). New York: Guilford Press.

Moore, S. F. (1978). *Law as process*. New York: Routledge & Kegan Paul.

Takaki, R. (1989). *Strangers from a different shore: A history of Asian Americans*. Boston: Little Brown.

White, M. (1992, October). *Reauthoring of lives and relationships*. Presentation sponsored by University of Iowa Marriage and Family Clinic.

Wu, S. J. (1994). *An ethnography of Chinese families in America: Implications for family therapy*. Unpublished doctoral dissertation, Iowa State University, Ames.

■■■

5

Using the Task-Centered Approach With Vietnamese Families

Walter Nguyen, PhD

Service providers are often frustrated by practicing psychotherapy with Vietnamese clients because Vietnamese clients tend to express reluctance in seeking help, drop out quickly, and see little benefit from counseling. Cultural barriers to seeking help include the stigma of mental illness, lack of bilingual or bicultural staff, absence of help-seeking patterns in the culture (Yamashiro & Matsuoka, 1997), and lack of accessibility of services. Many service providers, professionals as well as paraprofessionals, may wonder if there is an effective approach to counseling Vietnamese families that would better suit their cultural traditions than mainstream therapy. One such approach is the task-centered approach. The author has used this approach with both American and Vietnamese clients and believes that it has greater applicabilities and results in measurable positive treatment outcomes (W. Nguyen, 1994; W. Nguyen & Dockins, 1994).

Since 1975, more than 1 million Vietnamese refugees and immigrants have arrived in the United States. They arrived in four major waves. From 1975 to 1977, following the fall of Saigon, there were approximately 130,000 Vietnamese arrivals in the U.S. The second wave—so-called "boat people"—began in 1978, following the border war between Vietnam and China. The third wave began with the passage of the Amerasian Homecoming Act in 1987, when thousands of Vietnamese Amerasians and their families began to migrate to America. The fourth wave included former political prisoners and their families. After the collapse of Saigon, more than 125,000 Vietnamese military and civilian personnel who worked for the U.S.-sponsored South Vietnamese government were imprisoned by the government of the Socialist Republic of Vietnam in communist re-education camps. In 1988, both governments reached an agreement that cleared the way for immigration of Vietnamese families from reeducation camps. This latest wave of migration also included detainees and political prisoners.

Acculturation Problems

Matsuoka (1990) attributed problems faced by Vietnamese families to different rates of acculturation. Many of the earlier Vietnamese refugees were from wealthy, prestigious backgrounds and had previous exposure to Western culture. These individuals often spoke English fluently and possessed skills that had direct application to the American context or could be translated with relative ease. In contrast to this group were those from economically poor and uneducated backgrounds (e.g., peasants and fishermen) who had limited exposure to the American culture. Adjustment posed more serious problems for this group.

Lin, Masuda, and Tazuma (1982) classified patterns of acculturation into four categories: (a) marginality, (b) traditionalism, (c) over-acculturation, and (d) biculturation. The concept of the "marginal man" was developed by Stonequist (1961) to describe those who lived between cultures. These people manifest a high level of anxiety and inhibition, which results in isolation, loneliness, and frustration. Traditionalism is the strong attachment to and awareness of the culture of origin, which may reduce the feelings of loss and the impact of culture shock. The opposite tendency to traditionalism is a hasty effort to become acculturated. People who overacculturate become detached from their traditional support system and become excessively vulnerable. On the contrary, people who adopt the biculturation pattern of acculturation want to be able to integrate the two cultures.

Nicassino (1985) discussed three models of adjustment: acculturation, learned helplessness, and stress management. Acculturation refers to the change as a person from one culture comes into contact with another. Learned helplessness refers to performance deficits produced by past exposure to noncontingent response outcomes. Stress management depends on three major categories: personal resources, individual coping behaviors, and social resources. W. Nguyen (1994) found that social support has the strongest effect on the psychological well-being of former Vietnamese political prisoners in the United States. Thus, it is common that Vietnamese refugees and immigrants tend to move to locations with established Vietnamese communities to seek social support from fellow Vietnamese.

Vietnamese Families

As the newly arrived Vietnamese refugees gradually acculturate into mainstream American culture, they are highly affected by their past experiences in Vietnam. Families that migrated with many family members tend to struggle with numerous adjustments, such as adhering to new standards and expectations and clinging to traditional rules.

An understanding of the family system is especially useful for working with Vietnamese families to establish whether their family structure is traditional or acculturated. The extended family is one of the most significant differences between Western and Vietnamese social structure. Vietnamese families typically include both the nuclear family (i.e., husband, wife, and children) and the extended family (i.e., grandparents, aunts and uncles, and other relatives). Historically, these family members were often congregated under the same roof, but transition to the United States has had profound impact on this structure.

Acculturation has caused a change in this format; however, extended families remain an intricate part of the Vietnamese family system. Extended family takes on new form as a result of the refugee experience. For example, "pseudofamilies" have been created, whereby friends or neighbors live together and share roles and duties as though they were biological families. Family values that include filial piety and respect for age and seniority are still very much a part of the Vietnamese culture. This includes maintaining lineage and harmony bewteen generations. It is customary to avoid conflicts between child and parent or between younger and older siblings through deferential and respectful behavior. Filial relationships with parents and siblings are among the highest priorities of the Vietnamese culture (Matsuoka, 1990).

Basic Concepts of the Task-Centered Approach

The task-centered approach was developed by William Reid (1978) as a social casework method. This method is based on three key concepts: target problem, tasks, and time limit. It focuses on a target problem as defined by clients and agreed to by the practitioner. It uses tasks developed by clients with the help of the practitioner to achieve goals. Goals are measurable by quantities or level of intensity based on the baseline conditions of the problem. For example, a Vietnamese client at the initial interview defines her problem as feeling sad every day. A goal of treatment can be to reduce sadness to 4 days per week. Lastly, task-centered treatment is time limited, meaning between 6 and 12 sessions, or fewer, depending on the problem.

The problems that the task-centered approach attempts to reduce are "problems in living." They include (a) interpersonal conflicts, such as marital, parent–child, sibling, and peers; (b) dissatisfaction in social relations, such as lack of assertiveness; (c) problems with formal organizations, such as expulsion from school; (d) difficulties in role performance; (e) decision-making problems; (f) reactive emotional distress, such as anxiety or depression due to a specific event or set of circumstances (e.g., separation from a loved one, financial difficulties, or illness); (g) inadequate resources, such as money, housing, food, transportation, child care, or job; and (h) psychological or behavioral problems not elsewhere classified, such as habit disorders, addictive disorders, public relations, concerns about image, and thought disturbances (Epstein, 1992; Reid, 1978).

Task-centered treatment is an action-oriented approach based on the assumptions that talk or insight into the problem may not produce changes unless actions toward achieving goals are developed and implemented. What makes a cognitive event an action is the bringing about of something. Thus, making a decision can be considered an action because something has been accomplished. According to Reid (1978), the concept of action provides a better fit with the philosophy of task-centered treatment, which is to help people do what they want. Although one can modify a person's behavior without his or her knowledge or even consent, one can scarcely help a person plan and executive problem-solving actions without involving him or her in the process.

Task-centered treatment starts with the way the clients define their problems in their own words. It emphasizes the importance of problems *acknowledged* by the client rather than *attributed* problems usually defined by the practitioner or mandated by other systems. An acknowledged problem is one that the client has explained by statements about his or her problems that the client volunteers when asked or has agreed with when presented to him or her. Thus, to be considered acknowledged, a problem must be explicitly stated.

Treatment focuses on the client's *motivation*, meaning whether clients want to do something about the problem. For task-centered treatment, the interest is on those problems that clients can alleviate through independent action outside of the treatment session. The target problems need to be specific (explicitly defined and delimited). For example, to say simply that a mother and son "have a disturbed relationship" is not specific. The statement becomes more specific when the interactions that make up their difficulties are explicitly defined, for example, "they quarrel over the age of the son's girlfriend."

Effectiveness of Task-Centered Treatment

Reid (1978) suggested that task-centered treatment as a form of brief treatment is effective in dealing with problems that fall within the topology of problems listed in the foregoing section. Psychosocial problems generally reflect temporary breakdowns in coping that set in motion forces for change. These forces, principally the client's own motivations to alleviate his distress, operate rapidly in most cases to reduce the problem to a tolerance level, at which point the possibility of further change lessens. If so, clients might be expected to benefit as much from short-term treatment as from more extended periods of service. Placing time limits on the brief service might enhance effectiveness by mobilizing the efforts of both practitioner and clients. Effectiveness would be further augmented by concentrated attention on delimited problems in which practitioners, using traditional casework techniques in a highly focused way, would help clients formulate and carry out problem-solving actions.

In most instances, the model was able to reduce a set of related problems that clustered around the target problem. The model was less effective if the problem was broad in scope, that or loose in focus. Taken together, the research reports on task-centered work indicate that it produces satisfactory results over a wide area of problems in living. It is very efficient and cost-effective to clients (Epstein, 1992). It is assumed that because this approach worked well with low-income, American clients it would apply well to Vietnamese clients with similar socioeconomic conditions and problems in living (Reid, 1978).

Essential Techniques of Task-Centered Treatment

The strategy of the task-centered model stems from two purposes: to help clients alleviate problems that concern them and to provide clients with constructive problem-solving experiences that will enhance their willingness to use help in the future to enhance their own problem-solving capacities (Reid, 1978). As the name of the model suggests, the central strategy of the task-centered approach relies on tasks as a means of problem resolution. The success of the treatment relies on the practitioner's skills of task development, which entail anticipation of obstacles to task performance and interview techniques that follow a lineal pattern (H. Nguyen, 1988). The practitioner must urge clients to come up with tasks and must anticipate obstacles in the client's commitment to implement these tasks.

Although most of the tasks are developed for clients to undertake, the practitioner may carry out some tasks designed to promote clients' tasks or to secure resources that clients cannot obtain on their own. Because clients' and practitioners' tasks are carried outside of the sessions, a service contract needs to be developed, which will serve as a guideline, a reminder of tasks to be carried out, and a commitment toward problem resolution.

Appropriateness of Task-Centered Approach in Work With Vietnamese Families

For clients who express existential concern or who are in dependent states (welfare) or protective states (jail), who are opposed to structure, or who are actively psychotic or chemically dependent, the task-centered approach might not be appropriate. There is a goodness of fit between this approach and Vietnamese clients; most problems faced by Vietnamese families would fall into categories of problems in living as delineated above.

Of particular interest are problems relating to interpersonal conflicts, inadequate resources, reactive emotional stress, psychological difficulties, and behavioral problems.

The majority of Vietnamese clients are in lower socioeconomic classes and use and prefer a different mode of helping—one that is more structured, more directive, and places more emphasis on action. This is also the focus of task-centered treatment because the approach was developed to respond to the needs of clients of a social work profession, who tend to be poor and who are more open to advice (Reid, 1978). Although the core conditions of an optimal therapeutic relationship (i.e., empathy, nonpossessive warmth, and genuineness) do contribute to successful outcomes and should be used in task-centered treatment whenever deemed appropriate, they are not the essential conditions for successful problem resolution based on the task-centered model.

Case Illustration

When Vietnamese families seek help or are referred for counseling by a third party, they are usually overwhelmed by stresses and feelings of helplessness. Quite often they do not agree with the agencies or practitioners regarding what is wrong with them, yet they may not speak up for themselves. They either comply reluctantly or drop out of treatment. They may be labeled as resistant or impossible to work with. Using task-centered key concepts, the practitioner should encourage Vietnamese families to describe what they see as problems in their life that they want to work on. Sometimes it is a matter of rephrasing the problem in a way that fits the Vietnamese clients' worldview. For example, a 35-year-old Vietnamese woman complained of feeling very sad, irritable, and isolated. She cried every day and had sleep disturbances. She experienced difficulties finding employment after quitting a job with an electronics company because of conflicts with her supervisor. This woman expressed negative views of herself, the world, and her future. She also had suicidal ideation.

The client was diagnosed as severely depressed. Aside from encouraging her to see a psychiatrist for medication, the counselor used an insight-oriented approach in his work with her. This helped temporarily but did not seem to make sense to the client. The practitioner in this case did not take into consideration the fact that the client defined failing to find employment as the priority problem. Using the task-centered approach, the practitioner later worked with the client on how to find a job because this is what the client was interested in doing. The client implemented many tasks that she planned herself, which resulted in her finding a job. By doing the tasks, the client felt good about herself, regained confidence, and increased the level of activities that helped her cope with her depression.

In another case, a 40-year-old Vietnamese man was brought by his family and treated with medication and psychotherapy for some bizarre behavior, paranoia, and severe depression. The client lived by himself in a low-income, subsidized apartment and rarely went outside. Attempts to work on the client's issues of grief and loss, his depression, and other problems failed to bring this client out of his isolation because the client did not define his problem as the counselor did. Finally, the client said that he wanted help having a phone installed and enrolling in a vocational program. The defined task enabled the client to make slow but significant steps in recovery with the help of his extended family and interventions by the therapist (H. Nguyen, 1988).

Conclusion

The task-centered approach is appropriate as a problem-solving method for Vietnamese families that experience daily problems of adjustment to an unfamiliar culture. Most of these problems are concrete and can be phrased in concrete or specific terms. In general, Vietnamese people tend to respond readily to a task-centered approach, so it can be an alternative to other insight-oriented methods when those methods fail to help or it can be a treatment of primary choice.

References

Epstein, L. (1992). *Brief treatment and a new look at the task-centered approach.* New York: Macmillan.

Lin, K., Masuda, M., & Tazuma, L. (1982). Adaptational problems of Vietnamese refugees: Part III. Case studies in clinic and field: Adaptive and maladaptive. *Psychiatric Journal of the University of Ottawa, 7,* 174–183.

Matsuoka, J. (1990). Differential acculturation among Vietnamese refugees. *Social Work, 35,* 241–345.

Nguyen, H. (1988). Task-centered approach to working with refugees. *Refugee Mental Health Letter, 2*(12), 4–6.

Nguyen, W. (1994). *Psychological well-being of the former Vietnamese political prisoner in the United States.* Unpublished doctoral dissertation, University of Texas at Arlington.

Nguyen, W., & Dockins, G. (1994). *The cultural awareness series: Counseling the Asian-American.* El Paso, Texas: Aliviane NO-AD.

Nicassino, P. M. (1985). The psychosocial adjustment of Southeast Asian refugees. *Journal of Cross-Cultural Psychology, 16*(2), 153–173.

Reid, W. J. (1978). *The task-centered system.* New York: Columbia University Press.

Stonequist, E. V. (1961). *The marginal man.* New York: Russell & Russell.

Yamashiro, G., & Matsuoka, J. K. (1997). Help-seeking among Asian and Pacific Americans: A mutiperspective analysis. *Social Work, 42,* 176–186.

■ ■ ■

6

Exploring Aspects of
Filipino American Families

Rocco A. Cimmarusti, LCSW

Filipinos are the fastest growing Asian population in the United States. Yet, we Westerners know little about the Filipino American family, aspects of its organization, facets of its functioning, or salient cultural values. This chapter explores these issues in the first-generation Filipino American family and offers specific treatment recommendations and case examples.

As a whole, Asians are often seen as reluctant to attend therapy and instead receive such dubious praise as the "model minority" (Crystal, 1989; Sue, 1981). The myth exists that Asians adapt well to our society, are overachievers, do well in school, and do not experience problems. Asian children are stereotyped as smart and never causing their families any trouble. Generally, however, there is evidence that suggests that Asian groups experience problems in the same proportion as the mainstream population (Araneta, 1982; Sue, 1981).

Chapter reprinted from volume 22, number 2 of the *Journal of Marriage and Family Therapy*. Copyright © 1996, American Association for Marriage and Family Therapy. Reprinted with permission.

According to 1980 census data, the Filipino American population is the largest Asian population in Chicago and the largest Asian group in the United States ("Filipinos," 1990). A survey of 100 mostly first-generation Filipino American adults was conducted by the Filipino American Council of Chicago, Committee on Social Services and Human Resources, and with the assistance of the author. The results indicated that 39% of the respondents had experienced some sort of problem with assimilating into American culture, 32% had problems communicating with their children, 25% experienced a drug or alcohol problem with their children, 20% had a child drop out of school, and 33% experienced conflict between American and Filipino values resulting in family conflict.

Yet, first- and second-generation Filipino Americans seem rarely to use mental health and social services. A brief and informal survey of several Chicago-area social service agencies indicated that they served few or no Filipino American clients. However, according to the survey mentioned above, a staggering 80% of the respondents indicated that they would seek help at services provided by the Filipino American community or by clinicians who were sensitive to Filipino culture.

A culturally competent, family-oriented clinician, rather than an individually oriented clinician, would more likely be successful with Filipino American clients because the family is of such prime importance in the Filipino culture. The purpose of this chapter, then, is to increase the clinician's cultural competence for working with first- and second-generation Filipino Americans and their families. Clinicians should expect as much variation among Filipino families, however, as with any group of families and, therefore, should remain curious about the unique interpretation the family has made of the concepts contained herein.

The task of writing this chapter was undertaken by the author as a result of his experiences while traveling in the Philippines, his volunteer efforts with the Filipino American Council of Chicago on his return, and direct clinical practice with several first-generation Filipino American families. On a more personal level, the author was married for over 17 years to a first-generation Filipino immigrant. Although the accuracy of the author's remarks should be considered within the context of these experiences, the reader is reminded that the author is not a Filipino American and hence the observations that are shared are subject to all the possible misinterpretations of anyone who offers their personal constructions about another's culture.

Filipino Americans an Invisible Minority

One factor that contributes to the disparity between the need for therapy services among Filipino Americans and their use of such services may be the stereotype among mainstream Americans that Filipinos are well suited for and are already acculturated into American life. Potential referral sources may not think that Filipino Americans need professional help.

Perhaps this stereotype is partly a result of America's ignominious history with the people of the Philippine Islands. Though it is beyond the scope of this chapter, suffice it to say that America's view of Filipinos has changed over the years to suit the best interests of the U.S. government. The stereotype that Filipinos are well assimilated into American culture has colluded with aspects of the Filipino culture that, in the opinion of the author, have been both misunderstood and misapplied and have led to making Filipinos an invisible Asian minority.

One such aspect is that Filipinos have been thought of as possessing a "colonial mentality" (Araneta, 1982). This phenomenon, it is said, encourages Filipinos to appear to embrace American values, to make them look "Americanized." In all likelihood, though, this phenomenon is probably the consequence of the Filipino people trying to adapt to over 300 years of colonization and occupation of their land.

A second aspect may be found in the economic and political state of affairs in the Philippines. Because the Philippines are a poor, developing country that was occupied, until recently, by foreign military bases, Filipinos migrate from a country that suffers rampant poverty and the effects of foreign occupation (Friesen, 1988). With 50% to 70% of the population below the poverty line (Balanon, 1989; Mydans, 1989), even the middle-class Filipino professional has either experienced poverty or has been sheltered from it in her or his homeland. If one's reason for immigration to the United States was to escape such unpleasant conditions, is it any wonder then that he or she might be reluctant to participate in therapy, which might dredge up unpleasant memories?

Clinicians are encouraged, therefore, to have patience and compassion for the difficulty first-generation Filipino Americans may have with participating in therapy. Ongoing curiosity about how the client family has uniquely interpreted, managed, and responded to the factors described below should help the wise clinician validate the first-generation Filipino American's personal story.

Family Organization

The most important structural factor for the clinician to remember about the Filipino American family is that the nuclear family is likely to be part of a larger extended family system, or clan, which plays an integral part in the life of the family. Extended family is not particularly defined along patrifocal or matrifocal lines but will often include members from both. This phenomenon has been described as a "bilateral extended kinship system" (Ponce, 1980).

There is usually a very strong boundary drawn between members of the family–extended family and outsiders that contributes to and is supported by a valuing of privacy. The boundaries of the extended family not only include in-laws but also siblings, aunts, uncles, cousins, and good friends. The clan is the locus of identity formation, social learning, support, role development, and the first line in problem solving. As with many Asian cultures, the elders of the clan are to be afforded unquestioned respect as the leaders of the clan. In very traditional Filipino American families, for example, elders are ceremoniously greeted by the welcomer by placing the back of their hand against the forehead of the person greeting them. Additionally, kinship terms such as *lolo* (low-low') for grandfather, *lola* (low-lah') for grandmother, or *tatay* (tah-tye') for father, and *nanay* (nah-nye') for mother are used to indicate their special rank. It would be considered disrespectful for family members to fail to use such terms. Clinicians are advised to seriously consider the influence elders may have in the family system and their potential importance to the process of therapy.

The boundary around the clan, albeit a strong one, can expand in order to accept new members. For example, new members are formally accepted into the clan through the normal process of marriage or a child's baptism, especially through the symbolism of the godparent. The traditional Filipino wedding, for example, can include a maid of honor and best man and a set of godparents for the veil, one set for the rope, and one set for the candle—or eight godparents altogether. Clearly, any one wedding can signal a significant expansion of the family.

Through such events, the clan extends its network of relatives. Godparents become as much a part of the Filipino family as blood relatives. Though the feelings of obligation may not be as strong to more distant relatives, the Filipino may number as many as 100 people as relatives (Ponce, 1980). Any one of these relatives becomes a potential source of support or help for the Filipino family and thus also for the clinician who is willing to use these resources for therapeutic gain.

Ponce (1980) noted that respect for authority that is commanded by the Filipino culture does not simply imply blind authoritarianism and that the apparent rigid hierarchical structure is mitigated by other cultural mechanisms. For example, family members have the right to appeal to others in the clan who will intercede on their behalf, if appropriate. Additionally, the emphasis on and importance of duty, responsibility, and harmony in the family constrains those in charge from unfair displays of authority.

For most first-generation Filipino Americans, considerable effort, time, and money is given to reconstituting or replicating in the United States the extended family clan described above. Thus, the clinician is advised to regard the described family structure as the reference point for most first-generation Filipino Americans, whether or not the clan is actually in the United States. In some instances a member of the clan has migrated to the States with the understanding, and maybe even the obligation, to help the other members to migrate here. If possible, she or he will connect with clan members already in the States to benefit from the extended family support system. She or he will then begin the sometimes arduous task of working to bring the other family members here. Attorneys are retained, and dollars, time, and dreams are invested in the process, even though there is no guarantee of success. Clinicians may find first-generation Filipino Americans at any point along this process of bringing family members to the States.

Family Roles

The eldest children in each nuclear family are assigned very special roles, roles that are so special there are kinship names for them as well. The oldest boy is assigned the role of *kuya* (koo'-yah) and will very often be referred to as such by the younger siblings, younger cousins, and the like. The oldest girl is given the title of *ate* (ah'-tae) and likewise will be referred to in this fashion by the family. These roles demand certain responsibilities in the family, such as caring for the younger siblings, helping parents with chores, and often acting older than his or her age. There are also concomitant privileges as these children are to be afforded unquestioned respect by their siblings.

The importance of the *kuya* or *ate* does not seem to disappear as the children reach the "age of *majority*." On the contrary, it apparently persists and may continue to be a focal point of family organization. Older siblings feel free to express their opinions about matters within the younger siblings' family. As adults, the eldest children may have a special bond with their aging parents and may be regarded by them as protectors of the family's values.

Mothers and fathers have unique roles within the Filipino family as well. They also are to be afforded unquestioned respect and obedience by their children but are held responsible to the clan for the care of the nuclear family. Their parents, grandparents, aunts and uncles, and older siblings have a right to comment on the couple's parenting skills or marital conduct, though this right is sometimes not invoked.

Because Filipino culture places higher value on men, the wife is constrained from demonstrating her power in public (Almirol, 1981) and so will publicly appear to be submissive while the husband will appear to have control. On a day-to-day basis, in the better-functioning family, the subsystem of women in the clan will have a strong boundary around it, such that the wife and her mother-in-law, for example, can wield a commanding influence over the husband. Hence, the wife's sense of well-being is central to the healthy functioning of the family, and a wise husband is careful not to challenge her authority in a capricious or authoritarian manner.

When this is the case, there is often a balance struck between "ceremonial" subservience by the wife and "ceremonial" authority by the husband. Both spouses seem to reach some tacit agreement and maintain this balance of outward appearances so that the violence is minimal and symmetrical escalations by one or the other are avoided.

Yet this in not meant to imply that women in the Philippines or first-generation Filipina Americans have the same power as their male counterparts nor that such an arrangement does not subjugate women. Family violence in the first-generation Filipino American family can be a too-frequent occurrence as a result of men having a disproportionate share of power, and it would be a grave mistake for clinicians to regard this imbalance as only "ceremonial."

Therefore, clinicians are cautioned to remain curious about the woman's experience of this dichotomy between husband and wife. It is, indeed, real, but, as Boyd-Franklin pointed out (Bonecutter, 1989), it also would be a mistake to overlay American feminist values on women of other cultures. The point here is that in well-functioning first-generation Filipino American families there is mutual respect between the spouses, and the appearance of the male dominance–female submissiveness is reserved for public behavior. In the privacy of the home, there is often a more egalitarian approach to family life. The important matter here is for the clinician to be curious and culturally sensitive as to how this arrangement is experienced by the parties involved.

Values

The Importance of the Family

With much emphasis on, and involvement of, the extended family, it is obvious that there is a high regard for the sanctity of the family. Perhaps because of the rampant poverty in the Philippines, the cohesiveness of the clan is necessary for survival. Nothing seems to activate first-generation Filipino Americans more than perceived threats to family constancy and equilibrium.

Therefore, it appears that the arrival of new relatives is occasionally met with initial resistance by one or both of the extended families, as if the marriage threatens the clan's sense of itself. The clan must determine whether the new spouse and in-laws will become functional additions or act in a manner that separates them from the extended family. Although there are no outward signs of disrespect, the newest members in the clan may be the focus of family gossip for a period of time until the extended family accommodates to the addition and expands its boundaries to include the new members.

Because the extended family network is so prevalent and strong, the question arises as to how members leave the boundary of the clan. In the Philippines, there is scarce need to leave the family. If a person marries, the clan is simply expanded. Relocating to another city is done occasionally but at some cost to the persons who move because they are cut off from the support of their extended family. Immigrating to another country, however, appears to be a more acceptable way to leave, especially if the immigrant finds financial success in her or his new home and supports the family back in the Philippines.

Therefore, the leaving-home task of adolescents may be regarded as a Western phenomenon and often is a cause of conflict for first-generation Filipino American families. It is the experience of the author that second-generation teenagers can assert their individuality in a first-generation Filipino American family when it is quite clear that the actions in no way challenge or question the beliefs regarding the importance of the family. In the well-functioning family, once this essential belief is validated, the individual is free to experiment with self-expression and pursue individual interests.

Without this validation, or if the family is bogged down with any of the ills that contribute to family breakdown, developing individual independence may become a battleground.

With the cultural emphasis on the family, and because it is a predominantly Catholic country, divorce is not sanctioned in the Philippines. Unhappy marriages in the Philippines usually end by one spouse abandoning the other. The abandoned spouse is then eligible for the comfort, empathy, and support of his or her extended family but may endure varying amounts of approbation from the extended family, as well as from his or her own internal feelings of failure and shame. Therefore, divorced first-generation Filipino Americans are usually accommodating to American cultural values. Consequently, they are susceptible to feeling guilty or ashamed and experiencing a lowered sense of self-esteem. If, because of their own level of acculturation to American values, they do not feel these disturbing feelings, it is likely that other members of their clan may feel disapproving toward them and strain the relationship.

The Importance of Obligation

As in many Asian cultures, duty and obligation are an important part of the culture. It seems, for example, that the strong sense of duty helps maintain family roles. But in the Filipino culture, duty and obligation take on a special significance, partly because they are effective ways to manage a large extended family's varied and complex relationships and partly because they fit nicely into a Catholic belief system. Although, much could be said regarding both duty and obligation in the first-generation Filipino American family, the author's remarks are kept to a discussion of obligation because of its clinical importance and usefulness. The sense of obligation seems very strong in the Filipino culture; thus, the clinician is likely to see evidence of it in work with first-generation Filipino American clients.

There appears to be a value on reciprocity of benevolence in the Filipino culture. Individual behavior toward another seems to rest on the premise that doing good begets reward, and if someone does you a kindness, then you are obliged to repay the kindness. This concept is expressed by the Tagalog phrase *utang na loob* (ou 'tahang nah lou 'oub), or debt of gratitude. Although the Filipino's sense of obligation may also extend to an obligation to retaliate against those who do harm, the principle of *utang na loob* relates only to considerate acts.

Repaying a debt of gratitude will probably be very important among first-generation Filipino Americans, as it is back in the Philippines.

It is a strong social norm in the Philippines. Those few who do not repay kindnesses are regarded as selfish and shameless and may be ostracized. For most Filipinos, though, the kindness is quickly repaid. Repayment comes in many forms, including being added to the extended family clan, but the form of repayment seems to rest on how the kindness is evaluated by the person on whom it was bestowed. The form or repayment can range from the formal inclusion into the family, such as through the role of godparent, to a simple response in kind.

The principle of repaying a debt of gratitude can be valuable in the treatment setting. The clinician who acts genuinely kind toward the first-generation Filipino American family and who helps the family resolve an issue that it considers a problem will find that the clients eagerly attend sessions as if looking forward to visiting with their "friend." The first-generation Filipino American client may repay a clinician's kindness and helpfulness by having an interest in the person of the clinician and a commitment to the treatment relationship. The author, for example, still receives Christmas cards from some Filipino American former clients updating him as to their well-being and the like. Therefore, the clinician is advised to try to be as helpful as possible from the outset to better join the family.

Additionally, the principle of *utang na loob* can be used to resolve family conflicts and bring family members together. In a couple's strained relationship, for example, one person "doing something nice" for the other has the potential of activating a debt of gratitude between the parties that the clinician can use to increase the couple's closeness. The clinician can encourage repayment of the kindness by the initial recipient and create an ongoing spiral of nice acts between the couple, as each repays the other's kindness.

The Importance of Harmony

The outward appearance of harmonious relations is very important within Filipino culture. This one characteristic alone underlies virtually the entire structure of social relations (Ponce, 1980). *Pakikisama* (pah-key-key'-sa-mah), as it is known in Tagalog, prescribes the avoidance of direct confrontation. In most instances, direct confrontation is used as a last measure, and once used this measure often will end in violence. The cultural mandate for respectfulness demands that people act in a harmonious manner toward each other (Almirol, 1981).

Although the concept of *pakikisama* is much more complex than this author understands or has related to the reader, highlighting its importance here is meant to alert the clinician to be curious about it. For example, the principle of *pakikisama* will probably work against any clinician who tries to get the first-generation client to confront those people with whom he or she is in conflict. From the perspective of Filipino culture, it is not only improper behavior but it is also crude and dangerous.

Obviously, there is a high likelihood of culture clash occurring in therapy around this subject. American culture values the ability to confront directly; it is seen as a sign of assertiveness. First-generation Filipino Americans are likely to regard this with great apprehension and dismay.

Therefore, pushing the first-generation Filipino American client to exhibit an American version of assertiveness is a waste of time unless the client is genuinely Americanized, not just appearing so. Even then, the clinician should carefully consider what effects such assertiveness might have on less acculturated parts of the clan. The Filipino culture has creative ways for avoiding direct confrontation. The most important of these is through the use of gossip.

The Importance of Gossip

In the Filipino culture, gossip serves a major function. Known as *tsismis* (chiz'-miz), Filipino gossip is governed be a variety of social rules (Almirol, 1981). Gossip often strengthens in-group loyalty, for example, because it is often carried out in public gatherings and is almost always about those not in attendance.

More important, though, is that gossip is an intricate way to criticize, without causing open conflict, another's actions or values or impugn another's rise in social status when that person has been shamelessly bragging because it is done behind the subject's back. The person who is the subject of gossip inevitably becomes aware of the criticisms, though, when some family or clan member reports what has been said. Once the subject is aware of what has been said, he or she can use the information as an impetus to change behavior.

This widespread practice of gossip leads to considerable triangulation among first-generation Filipino Americans. The process of triangulation, so often seen as dysfunctional to Western-culture clinicians, can be successfully used by first-generation Filipino American families and their second-generation offspring, especially as it comes to their dealing with their parents. By successful we mean that concerns or complaints about a person can be relayed to that person without straining relationships or exacerbating conflict. For example, a family member tells another member about concerns or complaints she or he has about a third member. When the person told has an appropriate family role, he or she can relay these concerns to the third part in a functional fashion.

An appropriate role in the extended family for the go-between seems essential in predicting the success of the triangulation. When the go-between is older than the person being spoken of or has a higher position in the hierarchy of the clan, then there is a greater likelihood that the information will be accepted without dispute. Triangulating an inappropriate person can begin a battle between the parties that leaves the go-between in the middle of a conflicted situation.

It is fair to assume that there will be conflict in such large, close families. As the data of the earlier cited survey indicate, about a third of first-generation Filipino American families experience some form of conflict within the family, usually with their children. The wise clinician is advised to use culturally accepted ways to express conflict that do not threaten the cohesiveness or continuity of the family. When respectfulness, cooperation, and harmony are maintained between parties, conflict is managed productively.

Case Examples

The L Family

The L family was referred by the family advocacy program at a local military base near Chicago. The young sergeant said his family was referred for a family assessment because he and his wife were accused of neglecting their three young children. William, as we will call him, was a 25-year-old Caucasian American. The youngest in his family, he hoped to make a career in the armed services and was on temporary duty in Chicago. Marie, his wife, was a 25-year-old Filipina, the youngest in her family, and was working two full-time jobs in the hope of bringing her parents to the States. The couple met in Subic Bay, a U.S. military installation in the Philippines, had been married 6 years, and had three children: Renee, age 5; Sheree, age 4; and Mae, age 3. Marie had come to the U.S. 5 years earlier. They reported that the neglect complaint was the result of a "stupid misunderstanding" on William's part.

The children were left unattended, the parents claimed, because of a miscommunication between the couple. Marie often worked from midnight to noon, whereas William frequently worked from 6 in the morning until 10 in the evening. On the day the children were left unattended, William expected his wife home at 6, and when she didn't arrive, he left for work thinking she would be home soon. Marie said she told William she was to work overtime and not to expect her at 6 that morning, but he had forgotten. The children were left unattended and came to the attention of base personnel when Renee tried to take her younger sisters to school with her.

The clinician had little additional information at the outset and felt that the combination of the nonvoluntary nature of the referral, the type of complaint against the parents, and Marie's cultural values regarding privacy might combine to make the parents guarded and fearful. The decision was made to use the first interview to get the parent's permission to talk with the family advocacy social worker, to determine how much trouble the parents perceived themselves in, to determine how larger systems, like child welfare and command, were handling the case, and to join with the family and empathize with their experience of being called in for child neglect. The clinician also hoped to gather some information about how the family was generally functioning.

There was, however, something odd in the session that disturbed the clinician. In the family's transaction, he noticed that Renee seemed very apprehensive and reticent toward her mother. She played appropriately with her siblings but seemed to avoid her mom as if her mother were a total stranger. Sheree and Mae, on the other hand, climbed affectionately on their mother's lap, and Marie responded appropriately. The parents reported that these were their children, and the clinician queried them about their theories regarding Renee's in-session behavior. This question was dismissed by the parents, who responded that this was how Renee was, and the clinician read the response as feedback that he should return to this issue later when the parents were more amenable to such a line of inquiry. The family did, however, agree that this might be something they could work together on in future sessions. Afterward, the clinician wondered if Marie had abused Renee to the point of terrifying the little girl.

During the conversation with the family advocacy worker, several factors came to light. First, the family had been reported for child abuse at a previous duty station. The mother had been reported for leaving bruises on Renee on one occasion. Also, Renee was the adopted daughter of William. Lastly, the family advocacy did not want the clinician to just conduct an assessment but rather wanted the family seen in therapy until the children were no longer at risk of harm.

The family advocacy social worker had developed some theories about this family's and problems: (a) There was a great conflict between Marie and Renee and (b) Renee's taking charge of her sisters for 6 hr and preparing to take them to school with her indicated some level of Renee's dysfunction, because a normal child would not be expected to respond in such a way.

The information gathered from the social worker generated hypotheses for the clinician as well. First, the social worker did not have a sense of the oldest child's role in the Filipino family, which lead her to suspect considerable pathology in the family. Second, there was something unusual about the disengaged relationship between Marie and Renee that needed investigation. Filipina mothers are generally not disengaged from their children. If anything, Filipino parents are usually very close to and nurturing of their younger children until they reach the age of 6 or 7, when some of the role differences mentioned above take over in the family.

In this case, culturally sanctioned roles demanded that Renee, as *ate*, watch over her sisters while her mother was absent and attempt to provide for their well-being when she left for school. The fact that William did not naturally expect Renee to watch her sisters can be seen as an indication of the different expectations American and Filipino cultures have toward the oldest child in the family.

What was uncovered in subsequent sessions offered a way to understand the mother's constructions underlying the relationship between Renee and her. Renee was the offspring of Marie and an American military officer who reneged on a promise to care for and provide for them after he transferred back to the States. To further complicate matters, this promise was not offered until the birth father had unsuccessfully tried to cause Marie to have a miscarriage by getting her intoxicated and taking her on a dangerous motorcycle ride. In retaliation and in response to the spurned love, Marie tried to take Renee's life when Renee was a newborn, only to be stopped by her parents. Marie reported that Renee's very presence often reminded her of how she had been victimized by this man, and she would then feel enraged. Marie had never related any of this to anyone before and claimed to feel better afterward and more responsive to Renee.

Shortly after Marie went through this ordeal, she met William, who willingly provided for the child and cared for Marie. Because of Marie's sense of *utang na loob*, William's offer of marriage placed Marie in an awkward position. Even though Marie wasn't in love with William, she felt obliged to accept his offer because of her feeling obligated to repay his generosity. Marie reported that she became pregnant with Sheree and Mae in an effort to fall in love with William and believed herself now to be in love with him. Clinicians might be surprised by Marie's willingness to marry someone out of gratitude instead of love. Because of a combination of Eastern fatalism, Catholic guilt and sense of duty, and the cultural mandate to repay one's debts, Marie could view accepting this marriage as her lot in life.

In this example, the referring social worker developed theories about the family's problems that had potential for inadvertently doing more harm than good. The idea that Renee was quite disturbed, for example, ran the risk of supporting the mother's negative feelings toward Renee and could have further exacerbated an already estranged relationship. The second theory had the potential of destabilizing the sibling hierarchy. Believing that Renee should not have so carefully watched over her sisters while the parents were absent overlooked the role of the eldest daughter, or *ate*, in the family. Destabilizing the sibling hierarchy in a first-generation Filipino family in this way could have had the effect of robbing the oldest child of her authorized power and depriving the parents of a culturally sanctioned assistant. As the father was an American, he would have been appraised of the role of the oldest child in the Filipino family.

The T Family

This first-generation Filipino family was referred for family therapy by a psychiatrist who had seen the 18-year-old daughter during her hospitalization and was seeing her as an outpatient for individual therapy. The doctor felt that the family was "quite pathologically enmeshed" and desperately needed family treatment to let go of the daughter. The daughter, Sharon, was hospitalized because of a suicide attempt that came after months of acting out behaviors, such as staying out without permission and quitting school.

Sharon was the youngest of five children. The family immigrated in 1975, 2 years after the father arrived in the States, and each member of the family was well educated and had a good job, except for Sharon, who was employed as a cashier. She had dropped out of high school at age 16 but had passed her high school equivalency exam. The family seemed to be a very traditional family, with quite strong values around education, achievement, respect of elders, and religion. As is common with first-generation Filipino

American families of this type, when a child becomes a family problem, one possible response is to send the child to live with family in the Philippines for a period of time. The thinking behind this action is that the child can be better supervised and that the context there better supports more strict enforcement of rules. These families often view American parenting as lax and lenient, and American society and child protection regulations are seen as impediments to accepted strict child-rearing practices, such as spanking the child. Sharon's being sent to the Philippines for several months for an attitude adjustment failed because she saw life for adolescents there as repressed and dull. After several months, she returned to the States.

In session, she acknowledged feeling closer to her father than her mother, and her mother and Sharon seemed caught in a sequence of escalating conflict that primarily centered around what it meant to be a good daughter and family member. Her father seemed to be in great agony over the situation but was more distant from the conflict and thus more hopeful than the mother that the situation would improve. Other siblings were apparently uninvolved in the situation, and Sharon did not use them as a resource for intervening with the parents nor did they seem to be making any efforts to get Sharon to bend to their parents' will.

Rather than see the family as pathologically enmeshed as the psychiatrist hypothesized, the clinician wondered if perhaps they weren't enmeshed enough. It struck the clinician as very odd that the siblings were so univolved in the conflict. Apparently, Sharon had lost respect for her *ate* and *kuya* because she viewed them as agents of the parents, and they apparently had given up on her. Furthermore, the conflict between mother and daughter seemed very centered around the issue of inclusion. This combination of factors led the clinician to hypothesize that Sharon might be too isolated from her family. Consequently, she could not use the avenues for gaining independence that already existed within the family because she was incapable of accessing them. Unfortunately, her father's employment situation forced the family to discontinue therapy before the following ideas could be operationalized. They are offered to the reader as an illustration of how one might develop culturally sensitive ideas and plans with first-generation Filipino American families.

The clinician considered that therapy that sided with Sharon in her attempts for independence might actually do more damage than good, because it could result in a precipitated independence and activate the very conflict (around inclusion) it presumed to resolve.

The first moves of therapy with this family, therefore, would have been attempts to affirm Sharon's connections within the family and explore what legitimate means already existed in the family for gaining independence to solidify the base from which she could individuate. In other words, the clinician would have negotiated for each side in this conflict as he attempted to help Sharon understand that her rush to grow up would only work against her and also to help the parent understand that Sharon's behavior was influenced by American cultural values. Each party would need to find some way to accommodate the other.

The psychiatrist's hypothesis that the daughter was hopelessly caught in a pathologically enmeshed family could have inadvertently facilitated more harm than good by placing the child in the middle of an unworkable struggle between the parents and the doctor. Attempts by the psychiatrist to pull the child from the family would have most probably been met by the family's pulling the child back toward them, not out of resistance to change but rather out of a culturally determined deep concern that there are correct and incorrect ways to grow up.

Instead, a discussion between Sharon and her siblings as to the meaning of independence, the proper ways to attain it, and the benefits of taking such paths might have begun a focus in therapy that could culminate with including the parents in the discussion. Treatment would have thus avoided the actions of struggling over independence and instead become focused on how the various members of the family might agree on the meaning of, and methods for, achieving independence.

Miss A

This example concerns a 26-year-old Filipina who was referred to individual therapy for treatment of depression. She was the second of five children and had immigrated to the United States at age 8. At the time treatment began, she was living with a young Caucasian American man and was very concerned that her parents did not approve of her living arrangements. She also reported that she was not assertive in her relationship with her boyfriend and felt taken for granted.

In the initial interviews, Leilani, as we will call her, cried over any mention of her situation. She described her relationship with significant others in terms that made her sound as if she acted much younger than her age. When queried further, Leilani seemed more apprehensive of approbation from her father than her mother. The clinician hypothesized that this meant that Leilani was closer to her father than her mother.

Working individually with Leilani, the clinician was able to assess that the father's immigration to the United States was emotionally difficult for him. The father, who held important positions in the Philippines but had to essentially start anew in America, had more difficulty adapting than the mother, who was able to continue in her career and actually experience increased earnings. The father's consequent depression was most directly expressed to Leilani, and his pressure on her to achieve was increased. Once the father's critical and withholding behavior was viewed as an expression of his feelings of depression rather than as a reflection of some problem within Leilani, she was more able to risk facing him.

Two culturally informed tactics were used to ameliorate her parent's unaccepting stance toward her boyfriend. Capitalizing on the cultural mandate for harmony and using the acceptable methods for resolving conflict, Leilani was encouraged to use a go-between to communicate to her parents how much she valued the family and wished to remain a part of it. Her younger sister was used as the intermediary with her mother, and her mother was used as the intermediary with her father.

Leilani was also encouraged to have her boyfriend, Jeremy, attend family functions to facilitate the clan's acceptance of him. This young couple not only followed through on this suggestion but also invited their respective parents to a dinner at their apartment. This seemingly routine event was no doubt seen by Leilani's parents as a formal ceremony marking the merger of the two families. The first strategy also worked well, and Jeremy was accepted into the family.

Leilani became more assertive in her interpersonal relationships. She was able to continue working toward independence without crying, and she was more assertive with Jeremy. The young couple was married and were living in Hawaii.

Treatment Guidelines

First-generation Filipino Americans generally present themselves in therapy as polite, cooperative, verbal, and engaging people. They may agree to perform between-sessions interventions offered by the clinician, yet at the following session will have inexplicably not followed through on the assignment. If the clinician chooses to confront the noncompliance issue directly, the clients will often respond with great shame and attempt to avoid discussing the matter. Should the clinician pursue the matter further, the client may even drop out of treatment to avoid the direct confrontation.

Instead, the clinician is encouraged to take advantage of aspects of the Filipino culture to facilitate change. Because there is little in the way of therapy in the Philippines, for example, the first-generation Filipino American client will often respond to the clinician as if he or she is a medical doctor or clergy. The clinician will need to feel comfortable with being called "madam" or "sir" and other signs of deference. If the clinician allows or demands too much deference, though, it may create an uncomfortable and constraining situation: Clients may regard the too-formal or too-authoritarian-appearing clinician as oppressive and use feigned compliance to protect themselves. Even though respect of hierarchy and authority is valued in Filipino culture, too rigid a hierarchy or demanded respect is regarded as shameful, and opposition to it is appropriate. It is perferred for the clinician to develop a helpful relationship with the client, because the client's sense of indebtedness (*utang na loob*) may increase the likelihood of staying in treatment. The client's sense of indebtedness should, of course, never be exploited.

Second, action-oriented, in-session techniques—such as enactment, role play, and the like—may not be as useful as meaning-oriented techniques, such as reframing and circular questioning. Clinicians who are inclined toward these action techniques should carefully monitor the family's feedback during their usage. For some first-generation Filipino American clients, such techniques will appear too coercive and may result in these clients feeling disrespected. For others, it will not be such an issue.

Additionally, clinicians working with first-generation Filipino American families should look for ways to resolve conflict that tap the strengths of the Filipino culture. Religious beliefs, cultural demands for harmony, reciprocity of benevolence, cooperation and friendliness, as well as the strong boundary around the clan, can all be resources for the clinician and the family.

Conclusion

Filipino culture has a great and abiding respect for family and extended family that is central to the people's lifestyle and perhaps essential to their survival. Not all families are alike, however, and Filipino American families will use as wide a range of responses to life's stressors as any cultural group. Therefore, clinicians should expect as much variation among first-generation Filipino American families as with any group of families. Factors such as education, class, and the vagaries of life itself will impact each family's worldview differently, so clinicians are reminded to view each family as unique. What has been offered here is the author's personal constructions on first-generation Filipino American family life based on 17 years of living in an extended Filipino American clan, traveling to the Philippines, and treating Filipino American families. Still, these are an outsider's view and are thus limited; the individual client should be the ultimate source of interpretations about his or her own culture.

References

Almirol, E. B. (1981). Chasing the elusive butterfly: Gossip and the pursuit of reputation. *Ethnicity, 8,* 293–304.

Araneta, E. G. (1982). Filipino Americans. In A. Gaw (Ed.), *Cross cultural psychiatry* (pp. 55–68). Boston: John Wright.

Balanon, L. G. (1989). Street children: Strategies for action. *Child Welfare, 68*(2), 159–166.

Bonecutter, F. J. (1989, Spring). An interview with Nancy Boyd Franklin. In R. A. Cimmarusti (Ed.), *In context: The newsletter of the family systems alumni association* (pp. 3–5). Chicago: Institute for Juvenile Research.

Crystal, D. (1989). Asian Americans and the myth of the model minority. *Social Casework, 70*(7), 405–413.

Filipinos now biggest Asian group in U.S. reports census bureau. (1990, April 16–30). Chicago Free Press, *2*(22), p. 1.

Friesen, D. (1988). *Critical choices: A journey with the Filipino people.* Grand Rapids, MI: Eerdsmans.

Mydans, S. (1989, April 2). An Asian tale: Young girls, red roses. *New York Times Magazine,* pp. 44–67.

Ponce, D. E. (1980). The Filipinos. In J. McDermott, W. S. Teng, & T. Maretzki (Eds.), *People and cultures of Hawaii: A psychocultural profile* (pp. 155–163). Honolulu: University of Hawaii Press.

Sue, D. W. (1981). *Counseling the culturally different: Theory and practice.* New York: Wiley.

■ ■ ■

7

Important Considerations in Counseling Asian Indians

Winston Seegobin, PsyD

A review of the literature indicates that the Asian Indian population in the United States is growing and at present is the fourth largest Asian American group (Sheth, 1995). Asian Indians are often viewed as a model of successful immigration because the majority hold professional or technical positions and contribute to the economy (Helweg & Helweg, 1990). Asian Indian immigrants now "consist of college-educated, urban, middle-class professional young men and women of religious, regional, and linguistic diversity" (Sheth, 1995, p. 169). According to the 1990 census, there are 815,447 Asian Indians living in the U.S. (Sheth, 1995); however, little has been written and minimal research done regarding Asian Indians and mental health services (Durvasula & Mylvaganam, 1994; Steiner & Bansil, 1989). This chapter examines factors pertinent to counseling Asian Indians. First of all, the family structure and dynamics and their influences on counseling are examined. The roles of extended family and religion are also explored. The final section of the chapter is devoted to specific strategies and techniques that are important considerations in counseling Asian Indians.

Family Structure and Dynamics

The family structures of Asian Indians are in many ways similar to other Asian cultures. Some factors are unique to Asian Indians. An understanding of the structure and dynamics of the family is therefore crucial to set the stage for other factors and behaviors present in the family. In contrast to Western cultures, the primary focus of Asian Indian culture and religion is the family rather than the individual. Asian Indians tend to be group focused, or allocentric. Consequently, individuals are expected to sacrifice their desires and goals for the benefit of the group and, in particular, the family (Segal, 1991).

The roles of family members in the Asian Indian family are clearly delineated. The father is the head of the family, the authority figure, and the breadwinner. His role is the most important in the family because he has the final authority in most matters. The father's responsibility is to provide financially and to protect the family. In general, men are valued more and are seen as the primary disciplinarians and decision makers (Segal, 1991). The mother's role is a nurturing one. She is usually responsible for taking care of the children and household chores. In general, women are taught that throughout their life, they are to be dependent on their father, their husband, and ultimately their eldest son. Their major role is to get married and contribute to their husband's family (Segal, 1991). From a traditional Hindu religious perspective, women are seen as subordinate and inferior to men. Ramu (1987) cited Desai (1957), who summarized the status of women according to the Shastras (codes):

> Ideally, woman was considered completely an inferior species, inferior to the male, having no significance, no personality; socially she was kept in a state of utter subjection; denied all rights, suppressed, and oppressed. She was further branded as lacking an ethical fibre. (Ramu, 1987, p. 905)

Some Asian Indian families may not hold such traditional roles since migrating to the West. Therefore, it is important that the counselor inquires and determines where the family fits in terms of these roles. Asian Indians who were born in the West may have a more egalitarian perspective.

The principal role of children is to bring honor to their families by their achievements, good behavior, and contribution to the family's well-being. As such, qualities such as obedience, conformity, generational interdependence, obligation, and shame are highly valued (Durvasula & Mylvaganam, 1994; Segal, 1991). Children are seen as parents' pride and joy and the products of their hard work. One of the primary goals of marriage in Hindu families is to have children. The major role of parents is not focused on helping children become independent, but on fostering obligation and duty. The rule of thumb is that children are taken care of by their parents as long as is necessary, with the intention that children will take care of parents when they grow old. Steiner and Bansil (1989) noted that "children are considered the social security of India" (p. 372).

Asian Indian children growing up in the West may experience internal conflict between the collectivist demands of their family and the independence, individualism, and self-sufficiency valued in the society. Segal (1991) observed that these distinct differences in values significantly affect parent–child relationships and are most often evidenced in communication problems in the family. It seems that parents' recognition of these problems and desire to resolve them can assist children in their adjustment and decision making. Saran (1985) suggested that parents must recognize and realize that their children will not be the same as children raised in India. He further noted that:

> the lack of change in the attitude of Indian parents and their expectations based on the traditional Indian value system is a major source of strain among Indian families residing in the United States. In our judgment, parent-child relationships are the most pressing issue confronting the Indian community in the United States. Since most of the children are still rather young, the community has not, as yet, experienced very serious consequences of these conflicts. However, it is quite obvious that the issue warrants serious consideration from social scientists and mental health professionals as well as from the concerned parents. (Saran, 1985, p. 41)

This issue was quite evident in an Asian Indian family that moved to the United States on a temporary basis because their children were in an American college. While at college, the teenage daughter became attracted to an American student, with whom she later established a more serious relationship. Initially, the parents were accepting of the relationship. As the relationship grew, however, her parents found out that the man came from a divorced family and strictly prohibited their daughter from seeing him. To them, marrying someone from a divorced family was setting oneself up for disaster and disappointment. Thus, they threatened her that if she continued to see the man, she will be disowned and distanced from the family. At this point, the family began experiencing serious communication problems. Even her brother, who attended the same college, distanced himself from her. She chose to continue the relationship and talked about plans for marriage, which angered her family. As a result, she was excommunicated from the family.

Durvasula and Mylvaganam (1994) noted that "children of Asian Indian immigrant parents who become acculturated to American views of dating and marriage may find themselves in a difficult situation" (p. 101). They also observed that conflicts occur in families because Asian Indian parents demand that decisions about marriage be made by the family. For many Asian Indian parents, having their children, especially their daughter, become involved in dating relationships with Americans is very disturbing and a major disappointment. At times, these children are referred for counseling because of their "rebellious" and "crazy" attitudes and unwillingness to submit to the parents' demands about relationships and marriage. Counselors need to be aware of these tensions and issues when these families present for counseling (Durvasula & Mylvaganam, 1994).

Problems encountered by any member of an Asian Indian family are perceived as family problems. Thus, family dynamics around a problem are significant. This is clearly evident in the shame that results from an unmarried Asian Indian teenager who becomes pregnant. The parents, however, usually feel more shame than the children. Attempts to avoid shame can sometimes result in the family playing an "enabling role" in the client's problems. This was quite evident with an Asian Indian client whom I treated for substance abuse.

Doodnath was a 38-year-old man who belonged to an affluent family. He initiated treatment because he was addicted to alcohol and cocaine and often used the "family's money" to buy drugs. He was married and had one child. As a result of marital problems, Doodnath became divorced and later moved back home to live with his parents. His family, especially his mother, experienced much difficulty having the client in a residential treatment program. It brought shame to the family. Although the client responded well to inpatient treatment, he quickly relapsed after leaving the treatment center because his parents found it difficult to not give the client money because he was their "child," in spite of having been told that the client was unable at that time to handle money and it was detrimental to his recovery from drug addiction. They allowed him to continue in the family business and not inform others of his problems with illegal drugs. Eventually, Doodnath had a significant relapse. In an effort to cover the shame of drug addiction, the family did not adequately address the problems of the client after treatment.

For many Asian Indian families, marriage is a family matter; marriage does not take place between individuals, but families (Durvasula & Mylvaganam, 1994). In fact, it is not usual for the families to be involved in choosing the spouses. Arranged marriages often result. This occurred in my own family; both of my brothers had arranged marriages. I recall that as a 12-year-old boy, I was part of an all-male "team" that visited the home of the potential mate of one of my brothers. As we sat in the living room, the potential bride served us drinks and left the room. Discussions were held with her parents about her education and interests, but no conversations were held with her. Usually decisions were made after leaving, and they were relayed to the family. In some cases, spouses are chosen for children shortly after birth.

Extended Family

The role of extended family is significant in Asian Indian families. It is not unusual to see several generations living in the same house or in houses built very close to each other. Asian Indian families also get much support and assistance from their relatives. When children live away from their parents, it is not unusual for parents to visit them for extended periods of time. Relatives also tend to help each other financially. As a result of these behaviors, the Asian Indian family may be perceived as being too enmeshed and psychologically unhealthy. It is important for counselors to understand, however, that this closeness often aids the family in times of crises and also provides much needed social and emotional support.

Counselors who see Asian Indian families need to be aware that at times several family members may become involved in an individual's problems. For instance, when an Asian Indian client attempts suicide, many of the relatives, including aunts, uncles, and cousins, may show up for the counseling session and seek to be involved in the client's treatment. These behaviors should not be interpreted by counselors as "meddling" or inappropriate intrusions, but as additional support for the client. These relatives come to see the counselor because of their concern for the client. This behavior was observed at a drug treatment center, where several relatives attended family sessions because one member of the family was having treatment. Steiner and Bansil (1989) noted that when relatives of a patient who was hospitalized were permitted to stay in a tented camp in close proximity to the hospital, patient care improved because the family did not have to experience separation anxiety and remained integrated.

Role of Religion

According to Ramisetty-Mikler (1993), "Asian Indian psychology rests heavily on Hinduism, a 2,500-year-old religion, and on its strict social sanctions" (p. 38). Hinduism is a pantheistic religion based on the worship of many gods. In spite of their advances in education, some first-generation Asian Indians in America continue to hold to their traditional beliefs that their life will be happier and better if they pray to and burn incense for their gods. Saran (1985) also noted that religion becomes more important in family life after children are born because of attempts to maintain their cultural heritage.

The role of religion is affected by the level of acculturation and the length of time the family has been in the West. Although the majority of Asian Indians may identify with Hinduism, not all are Hindus. And even those who consider themselves Hindus may not be "committed" and may merely follow Hinduism as a tradition (Zacharias, 1994). Awareness of these factors is important because they will affect the client's response to the counselor and affect how the counselor addresses religious issues or the impact of religious issues on clients' functioning.

This author has worked with several Asian Indian clients who identify with Christianity, with some being leaders of Christian churches. It is rather offensive for these individuals to be labeled or treated as Hindus because they are Asian Indians. These individuals also have a completely different worldview. Therefore, it is very important for the counselor to check the religious background of the client and not make assumptions about his or her religious orientation.

Therapeutic Process

In therapy with Asian Indians, what information is needed to do an effective job and bring the desired results? It is very important for Asian Indian clients to see counselors as experts in the field and competent in their work. These issues can be addressed in the first session by counselors discussing their qualifications, degrees, schools attended, and skills. They should display their diplomas and licenses. It is also a good idea (and often reassuring to the family) for counselors to talk about prior experience treating other clients, emphasizing the number of clients they have treated. Asian Indian clients also want to know that their counselor can help them bring about changes in their situation (Paniagua, 1994).

Clients may also formalize the initial session by bringing letters of introduction and formally addressing the counselor. As treatment progresses, they may make the sessions more casual and talk about mutual acquaintances, common interests, and ask the counselor personal questions relating to family or religion (Steiner & Bansil, 1989). Counselors need to realize that these activities indicate that the client likes the counselor and that the therapeutic alliance is being strengthened.

When counseling is successful, it is not unusual for the family of the client to "adopt" the therapist into their family. Consequently, the family may invite the therapist to birthday parties and family gatherings, such as a wedding. Clients may also bring gifts to their last session or send gifts periodically (Sue & Sue, 1990). The therapist must be prepared to deal with these dual role issues in a tactful manner. The intentions of the clients are not to cross boundaries, but simply to express their gratitude. On one occasion, after successfully treating a client for drug addiction, his family expressed its appreciation by inviting me to a family get-together for Christmas. It seemed that the family's happiness over the client's recovery overcame the shame of having him in treatment.

Asian Indian families are also usually closed and private and prefer that problems not be discussed outside of the family. Therefore, it becomes very difficult for Asian Indians to seek professional help. Two implications are noted. First, counselors need to think of creative ways to get Asian Indian families into therapy before their problems worsen. Some Asian Indian families wait until problems are severe before initiating treatment. For counselors to work effectively with these families, they need to get them into treatment earlier. Second, when these families do come for counseling, counselors need to understand that they have come at personal distress and cost. Therefore, it is wise to acknowledge their difficulties and seek to help them in specific and direct ways.

Often the whole family may show up for treatment, even though the problem may apply to only one member of the family. In these cases, it would be better to work with the whole family. Children will often resist doing any intervention that will go against their parents because of the authority and respect awarded to them. Family secrets are often marginalized to avoid embarrassment. Thus, confidentiality is a major concern for Asian Indian families. A broken confidence is not soon forgotten and significantly impairs the therapeutic relationship. One of the issues the counselor may have to face is reporting suspected child abuse. The manner in which this matter is handled by the counselor is a significant factor in treatment and can affect the therapeutic relationship. Breaking confidence is often perceived as betrayal and may cause the family not to return for treatment.

Asian Indian families often perceive counseling as similar to a medical doctor's visit and feel that they go to the therapist to get a "shot" to make them feel better. Therefore, it is important for the therapist to explain the meaning and structure of counseling. Directive approaches to counseling often fit better with the Asian Indian's approach to treatment (Atkinson, Morten, & Sue, 1993). Time-limited therapy, such as behavior therapy, also seems to fit well with this population because Asian Indians often come to counseling with the attitude of "tell me what I need to do to feel better and I will do it." This may sometimes result in them rigidly carrying out instructions. They also experience difficulties disagreeing with their counselor, which may result in passive–aggressive behaviors. Asian Indians tend not to be assertive, and consequently, this can be mistaken as disinterest or lack of self-confidence. Resistance may also become evident when the instructions do not fit clients' worldview or tradition. They also tend to be traditionalists and act in very conventional ways, and having them do an intervention that is unconventional will be problematic. They also tend to manifest their psychological problems in physical ways. Thus, somatization disorders are prevalent (Durvasula & Mylvaganam, 1994).

Steiner and Bansil (1989) noted that when female clients are counseled by male counselors "behind closed doors," problems may arise for the treatment, as well as for the family. One of the ways these clients deal with their uncomfortable feelings is by suggesting that the counselor be seen as a brother or father. The counselor's assumption of these roles reduces the client's anxiety. Anxiety can be further reduced by parents' involvement in treatment by seeing the parents for part of the session. We need also to note that psychodynamic interpretation of the interactions (e.g., transference issues) can be detrimental to treatment because of its insidious nature (Steiner & Bansil, 1989).

Family Therapy Strategies

Marriage is a very significant relationship for Asian Indians. Even though the marriage may have been arranged, it is very important for the couple to stay together; divorce is rare among Asian Indians. As a result of the significance of them staying together, it is not unusual for Asian Indian couples to choose to stay together not for the satisfaction in the marriage, but because of the commitment and the children. The relationship between a husband and wife is thus based more on commitment than love.

Differences in how Asian Indians have been raised may sometimes result in marital problems that bring them in for counseling. This was quite evident with Anna and Jim, who were seen for therapy because of marital conflicts. Anna initiated treatment because she was feeling dissatisfied with her marriage. She and Jim were married for 4 years. Anna explained that Jim wanted her to perform certain duties that she had difficulty doing. Jim grew up in India and expected that his marriage would be traditional and that his wife would be the traditional Asian Indian wife who would cook and bring food to the table for him. Meiss (1980) noted that "the demand of the wife that the husband should help is a direct attack on his privileged status: for to serve the husband gladly and without hesitation is the highest duty of the good Hindu wife" (p. 914). Anna, however, grew up in the West in a home in which each family member served food for themselves. Consequently, when Jim indicated to Anna that she was expected to serve him food every day, she refused, which resulted in marital conflicts. Jim also wanted Anna to be the traditional Asian Indian wife in the way she dressed and her general behavior. She refused, and this resulted in even more tension in the marriage. Even though they were both Asian Indians, their diverse upbringing significantly affected how they saw their marital roles. Discussing their different perspectives toward marriage helped them in counseling.

It must be noted that Asian Indians raised in India have different traditions and expectations than Asian Indians raised in the West. Therefore, in counseling these couples, the gathering of background information, including family traditions and expectations, is an important first step. It is also important to find out how living in the West has affected clients' perception of the marital relationship. For instance, the changes husbands make as they accommodate to the West, such as performing household chores, are often criticized by their parents, and in particular their mothers, because they are perceived to have "lost their authority" in the home. Their male peers may also look down on them (Helweg & Helweg, 1990).

Wife beating is also a major problem among Asian Indians. Often this behavior is related to a husband's alcoholism. Women are taught that the responsibility for a successful marriage rests primarily with them (Helweg & Helweg, 1990), so in cases in which there are problems in the marriage, wives are blamed by society and their parents experience shame. Wives are often not allowed to work outside of the home and consequently feel isolated at home. Helweg and Helweg also noted that some husbands tend to be insensitive to the plight of their wives. The acknowledgment by the therapist of both the husband's authority and the wife's empowerment as a helpmate seems to bring a sense of balance and acceptance.

Working With Children

Ho (1992) observed that little has been written about the mental and psychological problems of Asian American children and youth. A significant consideration in diagnosis and treatment is the level of acculturation of these children and their degree of adjustment to Western culture. In counseling Asian Indian children, it is important for the parents to be informed of the children's problems and how they can participate in treatment. Gaining the children's trust as well is important. Usually children will be referred for treatment by an authority figure in their life (such as a teacher or a physician) or a trusted associate (such as a previous client). It is unusual for Asian Indian parents to initiate treatment without having previous knowledge of the counselor.

A counselor's knowledge of Asian Indian culture will definitely help in understanding the unique problems of the child. A thorough developmental history can assist in understanding the context of the problems. Additional strategies include the following. (a) See children as well as parents in each session. (b) Do not keep any secrets children tell you from their parents because they may tell their parents, who may feel that you are hiding information from them and distrust you. (c) Spend some time talking with the parents while attempting to find out about the problems of the child. Asian Indian children are often submissive and have difficulty relating to authority figures. (d) Engage in play therapy as a useful way to build rapport and confidence. (e) Understand where clients are in the acculturation process because Asian Indian teenagers may present with problems related to their level of acculturation. (f) Be patient with these clients, and whatever needs to be revealed will be revealed. (g) Incorporate the parents in the change process. Encouraging children to act against their parents' desires and rules is detrimental in treatment with Asian Indian children. These strategies can be illustrated with the case of Annie.

Annie was a 13-year-old girl who was referred to the author because of problems with stealing. She came from a religious family and had two older brothers. Her father was the youth pastor of a large Christian church. Her parents, who accompanied her to the first session, expressed concerns that Annie had stolen an object from another student at school and had shoplifted a few times. They explained that they wanted to find out what caused the behavior and how it could be stopped. It was quite clear that they were invested in Annie's treatment. For all the sessions, I met with both Annie and her parents. Initially, I met with Annie and her parents together for a few minutes before meeting with Annie alone to reduce her anxiety about being alone with me. Her parents indicated that they trusted me to meet alone with Annie because one of their trusted friends referred them to me. Initial sessions focused on building a therapeutic alliance with Annie. We talked about several aspects of her life, and I involved her in activities. Annie played with dolls and she was asked to bring them to the sessions. We also did drawings and talked about school and her relationship with her parents. The time spent with Annie's parents focused on assessing the parent–child relationship and attempting to understand Annie's behavior. After a few sessions, it became apparent that the parents were often busy with their jobs, and Annie was feeling neglected. Stealing was her way of getting her parents' attention. We discussed how the parents could spend more time with Annie. Homework assignments consisted of her parents increasing the amount of time they spent talking with Annie and also doing specific activities with her each week (e.g., going out for an ice cream cone). Annie's mother also became more actively involved in Annie's daily life. The stealing behavior quickly subsided, and the parents were happy with the results of the treatment.

Conclusion

Several factors affect counseling with Asian Indians. The structure and dynamics within the family determine some of the problems that occur within the family, as well as the strengths the family brings to treatment. An understanding of the nature of the family in this population aids in knowing what interventions will work and how we can make them work effectively. It is quite clear that families are usually supportive of clients and that extended families' involvement is a positive sign. Counselors need to be professional and come across as experts for counseling to work effectively. Although Asian Indians may have difficulties initiating counseling, when they come in, a directive therapeutic approach is best. For couples, knowing their background and family relational styles make treatment more effective. In working with children, it is best not to encourage any intervention that goes against parents and to actively involve parents in treatment. Saran (1985) noted that as mental health professionals become actively involved in removing whatever obstacles lie in the way of treatment, Asian Indians will be more open and actively pursue counseling in times of need.

References

Atkinson, D. R., Morten, G., & Sue, D. W. (1993). *Counseling American minorities: A cross-cultural perspective.* Dubuque, IA: Brown & Benchmark.

Desai, N. (1957). *Women in modern India.* Bombay, India: Nora.

Durvasula, R. S., & Mylvaganam, G. A. (1994). Mental health of Asian Indians: Relevant issues and community implications. *Journal of Community Psychology, 22,* 97–107.

Helweg, A. W., & Helweg, U. M. (1990). *An immigrant success story: East Indians in America.* Philadelphia: University of Pennsylvania Press.

Ho, M. K. (1992). *Minority children and adolescents in therapy.* Newbury Park, CA: Sage.

Meiss, M. (1980). *Indian women and patriarchy.* New Delhi, India: Concept.

Paniagua, F. A. (1994). *Assessing and treating culturally diverse clients.* Thousand Oaks, CA: Sage.

Ramisetty-Mikler, S. (1993). Asian Indian immigration in America and sociocultural issues in counseling. *Journal of Multicultural Counseling and Development, 21,* 36–49.

Ramu, G. N. (1987). Indian husbands: Their role perceptions and performances in single-and dual-earner families. *Journal of Marriage and the Family, 49,* 903–915.

Saran, P. (1985). *The Asian Indian experience in the United States.* Cambridge, MA: Schenkman.

Segal, U. A. (1991). Cultural variables in Asian Indian families. *Families in Society, 72,* 233–242.

Sheth, M. (1995). Asian American Indians. In P. G. Min (Ed.), *Asian Americans: Contemporary trends and issues* (pp. 169–198). Thousand Oaks, CA: Sage.

Steiner, G. L., & Bansil, R. K. (1989). Cultural patterns and the family system in Asian Indians: Implications for psychotherapy. *Journal of Comparative Family Studies, 20,* 371–375.

Sue, D. W., & Sue, D. (1990). *Counseling the culturally different: Theory and practice.* New York: Wiley.

Zacharias, R. (1994). *Can man live without God.* Dallas, TX: Word.

■ ■ ■

8

Connectedness Versus Separateness: Applicability of Family Therapy to Japanese Families

Takeshi Tamura, MD, MSc
Annie Lau, MD, FRCP

T his chapter; a product of the two authors' multicultural experiences, contrasts British and Japanese families in order to examine the applicability of the Western model of family therapy to Japanese families and therapists. Areas where the Western model is incompatible are identified, and modifications to fit the Japanese indigenous model are suggested. The most significant difference in value systems between the two cultures is the Japanese preference for connectedness. The Japanese person is seen as a part of the embedded interconnectedness of relationships, whereas British norms prioritize separateness and clear boundaries in relationships, individuality, and autonomy. This value orientation is manifested in

Originally published in *Family Process*, volume 31, pages 319–341. Reprinted with permission of Family Process, Inc.

the Japanese language, hierarchical nature of the family structure, the family life cycle, and the implicit communication style. Systemic thinking, which deals with the pattern of relationships, is valid for all families regardless of cultural differences. But therapists should note that the preferred direction of change for Japanese families in therapy is toward a process of integration—how a person can be effectively integrated into the given system— rather than a process of differentiation. An authoritative therapist style, the use of individual sessions, silence, and other nonverbal techniques are reactant to bringing about the desired change toward better integration of the individual with his or her networks.

A culture defines broad patterns of social order that locate human experience in a large context and legitimate ways of knowing and ways of acting (Cronen, Johnson, & Lannamann, 1982). Even though families and therapists are both affected by their cultural pattern, they are usually not aware of it because it is implicitly a part of their being (Lau, 1990). Cultural patterns come to light only to the degree that we can step outside the cultural systems in which we are embedded, for example, by comparing them with others (Watts, 1961, p. 23). Cultural difference becomes an issue when a cultural boundary is created within the therapeutic system, often when a therapist and a family belong to different cultures or subcultures (Falicov, 1983; Ho, 1987; McGoldrick, 1989b). The boundary can be within the family system in the case of multicultural marriage (McGoldrick & Preto, 1984), or in immigrant families where the degree of acculturation varies among the family members (Sluzki, 1979). For therapists from non-Western cultures, the boundary is created between Western theory and practice of family therapy and its applicability to non-Western cultures (Bott & Hodes, 1989; Kinzie, Sushaman, & Lee, 1972).

Family therapy is a topic of growing interest among mental health professionals in Japan (Tamura, 1990). The Japanese Association of Family Therapy was established in 1984 under the chairmanship of Dr. Koji Suzuki. There are around 800 members, of which 60% are psychiatrists, 30% clinical psychologists, and 20% others like social workers, teachers, and probation officers (Suzuki, personal communication, 1991). There have been a number of international exchanges between Japanese and Western professionals. Western therapists have been invited to give lectures or short training courses, and, conversely, Japanese professionals have traveled to the West for training. Numerous research studies are concerned with Japanese culture and family (Doi, 1973; Johnson, Marsella, &

Johnson, 1974; Kawai, 1986; Lock, 1986; Long, 1987), but few are related to the area of family therapy models and techniques (Bell, 1989; Colman, 1986).

The pitfall of foreign-trained professionals is a captive mind (Furnham & Bochner, 1986). After returning to their home countries, they tackle the problems of their societies with the knowledge, techniques, values, and solutions that they acquired overseas, without any attempt to modify these foreign procedures to make them appropriate to their own cultural contexts. Any attempt to apply Western family therapy models to Japanese families without considering differences in contexts will fail to achieve the maximum effect. There is also a danger that crucial information and, ultimately, engagement with the client families would be lost.

For the past 2 years, the authors have been engaged in a joint project in which they considered the challenges and difficulties of bringing together these two different belief systems in the therapist/family interface. The opportunity was presented by the first author's experience of being supervised by Western therapists in work with both English and Japanese families at the Institute of Family Therapy in London, England. The second author was not a member of the supervisory team around Dr. Tamura's cases, but was approached by him to help integrate his experiences at the Institute with his Japanese background. The two authors met on a regular basis, and the focus of work was that of attending to the differing world views and belief systems in the various interfaces. This article arises from a joint synthesis of ideas.

Some background information about the authors is relevant. The first author grew up in a two-generational nuclear family in Tokyo; both of his parents are from large extended families in conservative, rural Japan. He has two separate experiences of exposure to a Western milieu. The first was at the age of 17 when he spent one year in the U.S. as a high-school exchange student. He recalls attempting to identify himself with American culture without realizing what differences existed. His second experience in the West was for a period of 3 years in his mid-30s, after a period in Japan as a psychiatrist. During this time he worked in the M. Sc. course at the Institute of Family Therapy in London, and was successful in obtaining his Master's degree. On this occasion he felt able to stay meta to the two different value systems in a more objective way. He became interested in how the cultural pattern affected family structure, life cycle, and communication style. In his work with a team of British family therapists, he felt that the difference of the therapists' cultural backgrounds made a difference in their clinical approach and work with families. While learning about Western models of family therapy, he could not help raising these questions: How applicable are Western models of therapy to the Japanese context? Is it necessary and feasible to devise a Japanese model?

The second author is of Chinese origin and comes from a traditional, hierarchical, Singapore-Chinese family. Following secondary school education in Malaysia, she left to pursue medical studies and postgraduate training in psychiatry in Canada, including training in psychotherapy and family therapy. She has worked as a consultant in child and adolescent psychiatry in the British National Health Service since 1979. She is a member and teacher at the Institute of Family Therapy, and has contributed to the literature on transcultural family work (Lau, 1984, 1988, 1990). She has an active interest in helping overseas trainees to integrate their background values and experiences with ideas from Western family therapy approaches. Her current contact with Japanese philosophy and culture is through her links with the Sogetsu School of Ikebana (Japanese flower arrangement) where she has attained the teacher grade.

Dr. Lau is interested in the importance of attending to basic assumptions and categorical imperatives held by therapists that are ethnoculturally determined (Lau, 1984), and that influence their work with families. The bulk of her practice is with U.K. White families, but she also consults and teaches about ethnic issues that affect British mainstream workers and minority ethnic families, and that have an impact on public issues and legislation, for example, transracial placements and the Children Act 1989. As she is a Gantonese-Chinese speaker, she is often asked to do direct assessments of Chinese families of Hong Kong and Vietnamese origin. This has been especially valuable in contributing to the discussion between the two authors since traditional Chinese and Japanese families show strong similarities in a number of important areas. Both cultures have fundamental links with BuddhistConfucian ideals, including the organizing concepts of filial piety and ancestor worship (Lau, 1984). Family structure, which derives from these belief systems, is predominantly patriarchal and based on the extended family. Also, traditions and rituals, many of which have religious underpinnings, are to be found in both Chinese and Japanese families, celebrating important events in both the individual and family life cycle. There are also important similarities in individual and family developmental tasks through the life cycle, reflected in the way children are socialized (Lau, 1988).

Hodes (1985) and Lau (1985) contrasted two approaches to the study of cultural issues: a universalist and a relativist position. A universalist would stress the similarities of cultures on the assumption that they share certain basic rules and fundamental principles (Hodes, 1985). A universalist would assume that the similarity of the family process and the therapy model would overcome cultural difference. On the other hand, a relativist therapist would stress difference and assume that the family process is unique to the given culture and cannot be explained by any general theory, and that effective therapy can be carried out only by those who have enough knowledge about the cultural context (Hodes, 1989). *Ethnicity and Family Therapy* (edited by McGoldrick, Pearce, & Giordano; see also the "Overview" by McGoldrick, 1982) is a good example of the relativist position in its description of various American families of different cultural backgrounds. We believe in the universality of systems thinking in the sense that it deals with the pattern of relationships in human interaction. This chapter, however, assumes a relativist position in order to examine cultural differences.

It is always a topic of debate among anthropologists how ethnocultural boundaries can be punctuated. The case examples that we will present are of families from urban, middle-class backgrounds in London and Tokyo, and they exemplify broadly the comparison between families from Judeo-Christian and Buddhist-Confucian cultures, respectively, in which the differences between groups significantly outweigh ingroup differences.

Our main goal is to examine the applicability of Western models of family therapy to Japanese families and therapists. We set out the following questions: To what extent are models of family therapy that have been developed by Western therapists through their experiences of working with Western families useful to Japanese families and therapists? What are the areas in which the Western models are not useful, necessitating a modified Japanese model?

We first contrast the cultural value systems that inform the way members of the cultural group see themselves in relation to others, and how these values reflect on individual and family relationships, that is, family structure, family life cycle, and communication style. We then examine the extent to which these differences influence our clinical approach: how the cultural-value system informs the therapist's perception of problems, the desired direction of change, the role of the therapist, and the mode of psychotherapy. (See Figure 1 for a comparison of British and Japanese cultures and value systems.)

FIGURE 1
Contrasting British and Japanese Families

	Britain	Japan
Value system	Separateness	Connectedness
Worldview	Dualism (Cartesian split)	Holism (Buddhism)
Family structure	Egalitarian Nuclear family	Hierarchical Extended family
Emphasized relationship	Husband–wife	Mother–child
Family life cycle	Process of individuation Leaving home	Process of integration Arranged marriage Reunion with elderly parents
Communication	Verbal Explicit (maximize the difference)	Nonverbal Implicit (minimize the difference)
Direction of change (solution)	Differentiantion Individuality Autonomy	Integration Support network Sensitivity
Role of therapist	Third party "Neutral"	Connected directive, authoritative
Mode of psychotherapy	Verbal Talking through Therapeutic debate Externalize Unconscious → conscious	Nonverbal Meditation Silence Internalize Conscious → unconscious

Contrasting Japanese and British Families

Value System

In British culture, the importance of the separateness of individuals takes precedence in value over connectedness among the members of a system. The degree of individuation and autonomy of the individual are important determinants of a healthy family (Lewis, Beavers, Gossett, & Phillips, 1976; Skynner, 1987). The idea that humans are separate and distinct from their environment is an epistemological distinction that underlies most Western thinking about human interaction (Keeney, 1983, p. 110). Western traditional cosmology, which locates heaven and earth diametrically opposite, and the Cartesian dualism of psyche and soma are examples of a value system that leads to a view of the universe as a mechanical system consisting of separate objects (Capra, 1982). Growth in childhood, according to object relation theory, is a process of progressive differentiation of self from an attachment figure. Generational boundaries are supposed to be kept clear so that young adults can leave home and achieve physical independence from their parents. Since dependency tends to be seen as a serious problem, a child who cannot function independently by early adulthood is likely to be perceived as a problem (McGoldrick & Preto, 1984), and adolescent difficulties are often framed in therapy in the U.K as leaving home issues (Lau, 1986).

On the contrary, Japanese culture values unity and connectedness. In the Japanese traditional view, there is no absolute division of heaven and earth, nor absolute "onceness" of time in the Western sense. Everything comes and goes in cycles. Nature is a unity, and man is considered to be a part of this unity (Watanabe, 1974). Colman (1986) describes how Americans sacrifice connectedness to achieve separateness; Japanese, separateness to achieve connectedness. Roland (1988) contrasts the familial self of Indians and Japanese with the individual self of Americans. The familial self is the basic, inner psychological organization of Indians and Japanese. This involves intensely emotional intimacy relationships, high levels of empathy and receptivity to others, strong identification with the reputation and honor of the family and others. This enables them to function well within the hierarchical intimacy relationships of the extended family and community. The individual self, on the other hand, involves a self-contained ego boundary and sharp differentiation between inner images of self and other, which enables Americans to function in a highly mobile society where considerable autonomy is granted.

Japanese relate with others on the premises that they are mutually connected. It is like an identity whereby one belongs to a group that can consist of family members, classmates, or company colleagues. Americans seek their identities as individuals; being too closely identified with a group is tantamount to giving up one's identity (Hall & Hall, 1987). Herein lies the either/or dualism of the Western world view. The principle of the Japanese philosophy is holism such that any given entities are seen as a part of the wholeness, but the part does not necessarily lose its identity as a unit (Capra, 1975). For Japanese, it is possible for individuals to maintain their own identity without losing their identity as a part of the group.

The study of actual language used enables a therapist to understand the logic of the culture as well as the construction of personal reality and relationships between self and other (McGill & Pearce, 1982). Doi (1973) discussed *amae* as a key concept in understanding Japanese mentality. The closest English word for *amae* is *dependency*. According to Doi, it is a feeling that one wants to be loved passively, which first arises as an emotion felt by the nursing baby toward its mother. We prefer the term connectedness to describe the basic principle of relationship among Japanese because amae describes one's feeling, and its equivalent word, *dependency*, has a negative connotation in British culture.

There are some conceptual words in English and Japanese that do not have an equivalent translation and have to be expressed in roundabout ways. They often convey concepts that are not valued in the other culture. Privacy is such a word. Since there is no equivalent word in Japanese, in conversation it is pronounced with a Japanese accent puraibashie. The fact that Japanese did not have a word for privacy indicates that it was not a valued idea. But contemporary Japanese find the word useful, which indicates that the value system has changed and the concept of privacy is now more respected.

Most of the Western-inherited vocabulary has been used to indicate isolated parts rather than recursive processes (Keeney, 1983, p. 111). The concept of mujoe and ki, for which proper English translations are not found, convey meanings that are valued in Japan, but are not very relevant in the West. Mujoe illustrates how the Japanese regard the basic relationship between humans and the nature that surrounds them. It consists of a word mu, a preposition implying a negative, and joe or consistency; thus, as a combined word, it conveys an idea that nothing is consistent. It implies that the life of a human being is a tiny part of a wholeness, Mother Nature, in which one can do nothing but be part of the gradual flow of change. One is born, grows, and dies. One has no power over these irreversible changes. This value is seen in Buddhist teaching:

> Buddha exists only in one's mind, and the object is to attain the perception of the ultimate oneness of Buddha and one's mind. Once having attained this perception, one begins to see this world as does Buddha, or to put it another way, this world becomes that of Buddha. From this point of view, all things and beings in this world lose their objective basis of existence, as they exist only in ones mind. (Nagashima, 1973)

This leads to the view of an individual as a part of the web of interconnectedness, rather than a skin-encapsulated ego (Watts, 1961). It is of no use to pursue the trivial happiness of each individual. Happiness is attained when the well-being of the whole (group, family) is achieved. Excessive demands or assertiveness on the part of the individual would break the harmony of the whole. It is regarded as a desirable character feature that one can accommodate with others. A strong person is not one who sticks to his or her own views when meeting with disagreement, but, rather, one who sacrifices self in service to others and takes account of the views of other people (Bell, 1989). Accommodation is thus more highly valued than self-assertiveness.

The concept of Ki or 気 illustrates how Japanese respect the connectedness of relationships. It originally came from a Chinese word, *chi*, energy or life force. Since it was adopted into Japanese culture, it has taken on a unique meaning. It is a complex of concepts that include the Western equivalent of rationality, feelings, consciousness, will, and conscience. Doi (1973) defined it as the movement of the spirit from moment to moment. Ki is frequently used in various phrases and expressions of daily conversation. "Strong ki" means a strong will, "to lose ki" means to lose one's consciousness, "sunk ki" means being depressed, "pull one's ki" means to seek one's attention, and so on. The first author became aware of the uniqueness of hi when he saw a Japanese woman and her British husband as a couple. She had a good command of English. But when she was complaining about her husband, she suddenly switched from English to Japanese and asked the author how to say "Ki ga kikanai" in English, which literally meant that her husband was not making a good use of hi. Roughly translated it meant that he was not sensitive to others' feelings. She could not find the words to convey the exact meaning in English.

Ki can be conceptualized, in terms of the personal relationships, as mental or spiritual energy that floats around one's physical existence and fills the gap between individuals in relationships. A person who makes good use of the other personas hi can take another's feelings and circumstances into account when he or she acts or reacts; thus, the sense of connectedness is maintained without making each other's feelings explicit. "To make use of ki" (*Ki ga kiku*) and "to deliver one's ki" (*Ki wo kubaru*) are regarded as desirable qualities that make interpersonal relationships smooth by an intuitive, mutual understanding At the same time, an excess of hi is supposed to do more harm than good. "To turn they around" (*Ki wo mawasu*) means to be too concerned about another's *ki*, thus tending to misinterpret what the other person has in mind. Persons who "use too much *ki*" (*ki wo tsukau*) attend to trivial things about others and get easily exhausted because they unnecessarily expend too much energy.

Family Structure

The structure of the Japanese family was traditionally delineated by the concept of the "*ie*" system, which originated from the samurai class of feudal Japan. "*Ie*" literally means a *household* that consisted of a three-generational family in which there was only one married couple from each generation, together with their unmarried children. It did not include uncles, aunts, and cousins (McGill, 1987). Their responsibilities were to cooperate as a property-owning group in order to pass the reputation of the "*ie*" on to the next generation. Its boundary was extended to include dead ancestors as their guardians. A Buddhist altar was usually situated in the house so that family members could pray to the ancestors when they faced problems.

"*Ie*" families had clear hierarchy along the lines of gender and seniority. The senior male took the leading role, then came his son. The first son recruited his wife by an arranged marriage. The wife was supposed to leave her family of origin and to enter the husband's *ie*. The subsequent sons left the family and started their own *ie*. A woman was supposed to obey three men in the course of her life, according to Confucian teaching: her father in childhood, her husband in adulthood, and her son in later life. Senior female members appeared to assume a complementary position to the male members of the family, but they had implicit influence over the males and absolute power over the junior females. Thus, the newly wed wife, the newcomer to the *ie*, stayed in the lowest position of the hierarchy until her own son married and his wife joined the family. There was a popular phrase, "don't allow the wife to eat autumn aubergine" (a delicacy of the season). The wives could do nothing other than to accept and to put up with their position until they became senior.

The emphasized relationship is culturally defined, and any coalition with a third person outside of the emphasized relationship makes a perverse triangle that creates trouble (Hoffman, 1981). It is the husband wife dyad that is emphasized in Britain, and any coalitions across the generational boundary, for example, a child and one of the parents, are regarded as forming perverse triangles. In the traditional *ie* family, the emphasized relationship was cross-generational. The father-son relationship carried an important executive role, but it was the mother-child relationship that was implicitly emphasized and emotionally intense. Because mother was supposed to be the main caretaker of children, it remained implicitly valid all through their lives, even after the children married and formed their own households. The marital relationship became the perverse triangle and was left detached, particularly in the early stage of a marriage while the husband's loyalty to his parents remained strong. The wife, unsupported by her husband, inevitably sought her own support from her children. Consequently, motherchildren relationships remained intense until later life, which made it difficult for children to form close-enough marital coalitions of their own. In this way, the pattern of emphasized relationships was perpetuated in following generations.

The hierarchical nature of the family structure was congruent with the value systems of the pre-war Japan, albeit not ideal. The *ie* system was socially accepted and reinforced by the law until World War II. But a dilemma is posed when the value system of a particular culture is challenged by another (DiNicola, 1985). After the war, traditional values were challenged by American influences and by rapid industrialization. The concept of the nuclear family was introduced. People of the new generation acquired egalitarian value systems through a Western-modeled education, and enjoyed the freedom of individuality. At the same time, the family myth was inevitably passed on to them from the previous generation. They were often caught in the double standard of value systems that contradicted each other and created an impossible task of maintaining two sets of emphasized relationships. (This will be graphically illustrated later in Case 2.)

Family Life Cycle

Human growth and the family life cycle is considered in Britain as a process of individuation. For the Japanese, the family life cycle involves transition from one form of integration to another. Individuals never leave home in the British sense. Young adults often stay with their parents until marriage, even if it is financially feasible for them to leave. Those who hold the traditional *ie* value may stay with their parents all through their lives by recruiting a wife.

A marriage can also be considered as a process of integration leading to the more complex family system, which includes inlaw relationships, rather than as a process of individuation and separation. Major tasks of a marriage in any culture are the formation of a secure marital relationship and the realignment of relationships with the members of the extended families of both spouses (McGoldrick, 1989a, 1989b). It is complicated and difficult for Japanese couples to achieve both because relationship with the extended family is more emphasized. In Japan, there is a popular phrase: "A distance where soup does not get cold"; that is, the ideal distance between the parents' and children's households would be a few blocks away where they can easily deliver foods without the soup getting cold. The soup would be too hot if the two generations live together, but too cold if they live far apart.

An arranged marriage is a good example of Japanese ritual and the way connectedness is maintained through the marital transition. Although it is gradually decreasing, a third of the Japanese still meet their partners by arranged settings (Kamiko & Masuda, 1981). A matchmaker is called a *nakohdo*, literally, a middle man who takes a crucial role in introducing, negotiating, and ceremonializing (Vogel, 1967). There are many variations in the role of matchmaker, but the typical case goes as follows. A nakohdo is usually a person of middle age or above who is respected in the community. At the arranged meeting, the nakohdo introduces the marriage candidates to each other as well as their parents, who are usually present. After a couple of dates, the prospective partners decide either to marry or not, and so inform their partner. If they find it difficult to say "no" directly to the partner, they can alternatively tell the nakohdo, who would then inform the other party. The nakohdo also acts as a marriage counselor whom the partners would consult for their marital problems. In this way, the nakohdo insures connectedness between the two families so that they can avoid the direct confrontation of disagreement and the risk of losing face. The matchmaker's role as a mediator is extremely crucial. Mediation is a concept that characterizes the negotiating process at every level of system and organization in Japanese society.

Another important milestone of the Japanese family life cycle comes later when elder parents are reunited with their child's family. Most people believe that if one of the parents becomes physically weak, the two generations should live together (McGill, 1987). The timing of the joining often occurs when one member of the old couple dies or becomes ill. The major difficulties of reunion depend on the life-cycle stage of both parties. The aged parent has to accept the loss of the partner and the decline of his or her physical strength. It is often a difficult task for the old people to accommodate to a different environment and to new relationships. Their children are middleaged and their grandchildren are adolescents or young adults. The wisdom and support of the aged can be positively welcomed, but the elderly can also be a burden for the family in that they have to be taken care of, especially when they are physically not well.

Communication

Overt, explicit, and open communication is positively valued in the West (Lock, 1986). The sender of the message holds the key to successful communication by being clear and articulate. In a hypothetical situation in which two people are having a dialogue and the receiver of the message does not understand the sender's message, the receiver would say, "I do not understand." It is regarded as the receiver's responsibility to make the sender understand that the receiver does not understand. Then it would be the sender's responsibility to speak more clearly, for instance, to use another expression so that the receiver would understand.

In contrast, indirect and implicit expression is common among Japanese, Chinese, Malaysian, and other Eastern cultures (Hong, 1989; Lau, 1986; Shon & Ja, 1982). Indirect means of communication include frequent allusions to proverbs and folk parables. Japanese are not encouraged to make their desires explicit to others. Instead, they are expected to be highly sensitive to what other people have in their minds despite the minimal use of verbal interaction. It reflects on the structure of the language itself that, grammatically, the subject is often absent or left vague, which can be contrasted with that of English in which the subject is first and explicit (McGill, 1987). Successful communication depends on the receiver's intuition (Nagashima, 1973). If the receiver does not understand the sender's message, the receiver would look a little puzzled but would not immediately say, "I do not understand." The receiver would let the conversation flow a bit more fully, using intuitive capacities to try to understand the message because it is his or her responsibility to sense the message. Furthermore, it is the sender's responsibility to know by the receiver's facial expression or t he way the dialogue flows that the receiver does not understand.

Direct and explicit communication inevitably in Eastern cultures, in general, leads to differentiation between people. Assertive and articulate communication is often devalued and regarded as if the speaker were acting only on his or her own behalf, that is, selfishly and indifferent to maintaining group harmony. It may result in confrontation, leading to loss of face within the group (Lau, 1986; McGoldrick, 1982). On the other hand, indirect and covert communication creates a strong bond between speaker and listener. It respects a person's judgment about her or his understanding of the context in the dialogue. If one is explicitly criticized or ordered by others, self-autonomy and independence would be threatened and one loses face. If people take the initiative in understanding the context in which they are being criticized or ordered without needing an explicit message, they can stay close to others without feeling threatened. One way to guarantee autonomy and independence is by physically separating from the other, which is often the British solution. Another way, which is popular among Japanese, is by the use of a covert and intuitive communication style. These ideas are put into practice via socialization practices at home and at school. They also reflect the childhood experiences of both authors.

The following vignette shows the differences in communication styles that are widely accepted in Britain and Japan:

A British couple in their 40s came for therapy with a marital problem. The husband was physically violent toward his wife. The wife said he would not communicate, and often became furious and hit her if she raised her voice. The husband said his wife did not listen, and was more violent than he was with words. The therapist asked them to write on a piece of paper one thing that they wanted to say most to each other. She wrote, "I should like to be friends again if I could be assured of fairness in financial matters and that there would be an end to violent and moody behavior." He wrote, "Why do you dislike me so much?"

The therapist then joined the supervision group for discussion. The main concern of the team was the pattern of interaction between the couple, which had repeatedly led to violence. The European members of the team focused on the husband's depressed manner and ineffective message. The Japanese therapist's focus was on the wife, noting that she was verbally aggressive and very demanding, but his comment was not convincing to the team.

Therapists are likely to pick up the information that is different from their culturally defined expectation of meaningful observation. In other words, the information to which little attention was paid carried the pattern of behavior that was congruent to the observer's belief system. The wife was talkative, always using "I," not very keen to understand the partner, and she tried hard to be assertive and clear, which resonates to the normative communication style in Britain. The husband's communication, compared to his wife's, was quiet, obscure, very brief, and referring to "you" instead of "I," resonating with the Japanese style of communication.

The British therapists wanted to encourage the couple, especially the husband, to make their own messages clear and explicit so that each could be more aware of what the other partner expected in the couple relationship. The Japanese therapist, on the other hand, wanted to focus on each partner's sensitivity to the other, so that each could understand the other person's expectations and wishes. This was a reflection of the different emphasis originating from the different belief systems about ideal modes of functioning and behavior in the couple relationship; hence, a difference emerged in therapeutic aims.

Clinical Implications

Direction of Change

Goals of therapy are determined by therapists' cultural values (Kinzie et al., 1972). British therapists are more likely to define human growth as a process of differentiation, and look for ways to enable individuals to become more independent and autonomous. Problems are often perceived as resulting from excessive connectedness (enmeshment), or inadequate achievement in the normative processes of differentiation and separation. This might include a child being unable to leave home or parents not able to let go, codependency between partners not able to be self-sufficient, and unresolved bereavement where the bereaved still hangs onto the significant loss. The whole body of research on expressed emotion (EE) shows that high EE in a family, at the time of hospital discharge, predicts a higher rate of relapse in schizophrenics (Brown, Monch, Carstairs, & Wing, 1962). The premises of the research indicate a value in Britain that highlights the negative effect of family overinvolvement as an unnecessary intrusion into the achievement of independence. It relates to what McGill and Pearce (1982) call hyperindividualism—that British Americans "tend to be good at selfreliance, self-sufficiency, and self-control, and rather less good at maintaining mutually giving relationships, tolerating dependency, and integrating and expressing emotional experience" (p. 458).

Problem solving in Britain is often directed toward increasing separation. Thus, independence and differentiation are the goals to be facilitated. For example, the schizophrenics in high-EE families should reduce the face-to-face contacts with highly involved relatives (Vaughn & Leff, 1976). Bowen's (1978) notion of differentiation of self as the most important goal of family therapy aims to free the individual from stuck relationships and irrational social controls. Mourning work is to help the bereaved person differentiate from stuck feelings or unresolved mourning

In Japan, the "right" balance of separateness/connectedness is defined much more toward the connected side of the continuum than in Britain. A problem is more likely to be defined as a result of insufficient integration of connectedness, for example, when a significant member of the family is absent, when there is too much distance in the marital relationship, or when individuals are isolated from the support network. To achieve connectedness in the family system, notions like mutual support, sensitivity to others, and maintenance of group harmony become important.

The following case was seen by the first author, with English therapists making up the supervision team. It illustrates how the difference between the British and the Japanese value systems lead to differences in the perception of the problem and its solution.

Case 1. A Japanese couple, both in their late 30s, had been in England for 2 years with their 10-year-old daughter. They sought therapy for the wife's "depression." She could not sleep well, particularly early in the morning She worried about small things, especially when she had nothing to do during the day. She did not like to be in England because she had nothing to do. She did not speak English well, had few friends, and felt left alone all day. She did not go out often and felt empty. Her daughter was away at school most of the day, and her husband was busy with his work as an international businessman and did not come home until late at night. She was depressed previously when they lived in the United States, but not as seriously as now. Her daughter was then of preschool age, 80 she thought that her presence at home saved her from loneliness.

The British supervisory team was concerned at the husband's "overcommitment" to his work, in that he had to work extremely long hours. They regarded his flat facial expression as a sign of depression. The team hypothesized that the husband was caught in the dilemma of loyalty to his family or to his work. He had to work hard to bring in money to insure the happiness of his family, but his wife was unhappy at being left alone. If he spent more time with his family, he had to cut his working hours which, in the long run, could bring unhappiness to the family because it would likely prejudice his standing at work. The team postulated that the wife's symptoms served to protect her husband from becoming depressed, and she was offering a solution to this problem.

By the third session, they had had to cancel two appointments because of the husband's work commitments. In the following session, the first author shared the team's hypothesis with the family as a metaphor of two marriages. He delivered a message, stating that it came from his European colleagues, that the wife might think her husband was more married to his job than to her. The husband responded that he did not understand the point the team was making because "your colleagues are thinking in the European way." Then he explained the importance of his role in the company and said that his wife understood the situation. His wife agreed with him that it was not a matter of priority, and she took his work commitment for granted because they had no choice about it.

The team had posed a dilemma of change (Papp, 1983) to create a therapeutic debate between the therapist and the family, which might hopefully change the family's perception of the problem and the solution, but it was denied by the family. The husband may have felt that the message represented a "European" way of thinking because it suggested that marriage and work were subjective entities that one had to be loyal to, or that one could deliberately choose to make a relationship with. For the team, the premise was that the relationships between him and his wife or work existed only because he made an effort to commit himself to them. The relationships would cease to exist if he were to cease this effort. In Western cultures, individuality is the prime value, and relatedness is secondary in the sense that a person has the choice of whether to make certain relationships with other entities or not. For the Japanese, relatedness is the prime value. In this case, the marriage and the work were not the subjects of continuing effort toward commitment. Once the husband had formed a relationship with his work or his wife, he became an integrated part of the relationship and did not have to make an effort to keep the relationships. The relationship continued to exist in its own right. Individuality, therefore, is a lesser value than relatedness.

An alternative hypothesis in this case, which was congruent with the Japanese value system, was based upon the concept of the support network system (Landau, 1982). It was assumed that the husband was perceived as not sufficiently available. His wife, after all, was in an isolated situation in a foreign country where a sufficient familial and social network were not available. Their relationship was rather traditional in the sense that the motherchild relationship was emphasized and the marital coalition came secondary. If she had been in Japan, the major part of her support would have come from her family of origin and her own female friends. She and her husband needed to negotiate their relationships to adjust to their situation overseas. She suffered more from the lack of support networks in England than did her husband, who secured support from his workplace where he spent most of the day. She was totally cut off from the world. The fact that he had a job and spoke English, while she had no job and a poor command of English, inevitably put her in the complementary position. The focus of the intervention was to help them negotiate a different way of organizing their available time together so that they could provide each other with more effective emotional support. It was interesting to note that the intervention, as the outcome of the alternative hypothesis, was similar to that derived from the original hypothesis made by the British team, namely, posing a dilemma. Only the meanings attached to the observed behaviors were different. The British therapists saw it as a dilemma of choice, while the Japanese therapist presented the problem as one that required restoration of social supports, which were deficient in the wife's social support system. The "Japanese" solution therefore was one that emphasized integration. The "British" solution came across to both the Japanese therapist and the Japanese family as overly differentiating and, hence, alien.

The next case example (see Figure 2), which the first author had seen with a Japanese therapeutic team, illustrates how the hierarchical nature of Japanese families can become problematic, and how the solution has to be in line with the value system in order for it to be acceptable and useful.

Case 2. Aya, age 14, had been anorectic and refusing to go to school for more than a year. Her family consisted of father in his early 60s, mother in her early 50s, and Aya as the only child. Aya was very close to her mother and distant from father. She did not want father to see her nagging her mother. When she was depressed, therefore, she dictated to her mother by demanding that they both go to another room if her father were present, so that she could nag her mother without father's presence. Aya and her mother regularly took a bath together, which often ended up in fighting. In fact, the three of them slept in the same room, Aya being in the middle of the parents. She and her mother stayed close together while her father slept quite apart from them.

Mother complained that her husband had been a "very calm type" and "not good at expressing in words" since the beginning of their

FIGURE 2
Case 2

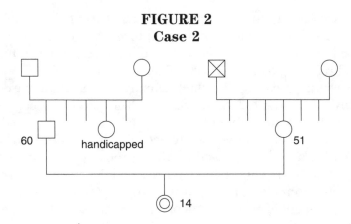

marriage, so she could not figure out what he had on his mind. Mother did the most of talking in the sessions, while father remained quiet, although he did respond from time to time in a very soft and obscure manner. His wife often spoke for him.

Mother was from a big family in the west part of Japan, far from where they lived. She lived with her mother, after her father died early and her two sisters had left home for marriage, until she married at the age of 29. They had an arranged marriage. She felt lonely being with a very quiet husband and away from her family of origin.

For over 20 years since their marriage, they lived next door to father's family of origin, which consisted of his parents and his sister. His sister was single and physically handicapped. They had a long-standing dispute with father's family of origin. When the parents got married, father's parents offered them a new house next to their house on the same property. Father's parents also gave him the property rights of both houses. Father's parents changed their minds when they realized that their handicapped daughter was likely to remain single, and demanded that father should transfer a part of his property to his handicapped sister so that she could have a share of the inheritance. Mother's parents offered financial support so that the couple could move to a new place to avoid the conflict. Father could not make up his mind either to move or to return the property rights back to his sister.

Mother was on very bad terms with her in-laws. Father's parents refused to speak to her, and accused her in front of Aya and her father of being responsible for Aya's problem because of inadequate parenting. Mother commented that Aya knew about her frustration, and that she wanted her husband to take more responsibility and to say what was necessary.

In a session, mother was asked to sculpt her family, including the parents of both sides. In the sculpture, she positioned herself next to her husband, side by side, and her dead father in back of her and reaching toward her shoulder with his hand.

This was a typical case in which a family was caught in the double standard of conflicting value systems. The parents accepted the concept of *ie* to the extent of staying in a house adjacent to that of father's parents, but not enough to accept living in the same household. Father's parents passed all their property to their first son according to the *ie* values, but later realized their *ie* was dissolving and wanted to reclaim a part of the property so that their unmarried daughter could be independent. Father was expected to be loyal to both his parents (traditional value) and to his wife (modern value). If he allied with his wife by moving away, he would be disloyal to his parents. He would be disloyal to his wife if he allied with his parents by complying with their views about the property. His only choice was to stay mute, to avoid this impossible dilemma.

The British therapists, believing individuation to be the goal of maturation and a marital relationship as the most important coalition, would regard the function of Aya's symptoms as calibrating the marital relationship. They might help the couple to create a proper boundary around the nuclear family. It would be a desirable process of differentiation and individuation if father, as a result of the therapy, solved the dilemma by separating from his parents.

Japanese therapists would take both cross-generational and spousal relationships as equally of prime importance. They would regard the function of Aya's symptom as calibrating the entire set of relation ships in the extended family, that is, getting her parents closer and rendering the grandparents more distant. The team thought it was equally important to create a proper boundary around the nuclear family and at the same time to maintain the integration of the whole kinship system. They thought the possibility of including father's parents and sister in the following sessions was premature at that point— although it would possibly create a dramatic change— because it would be too confronting and stressful for everyone and might lead to a disastrous separation from the in-law relationships. The team planned not to challenge the relationships with the family of origin, but, instead, to help father take a more active role in the family. The therapist connoted the role of father as that of a middle-rank businessman in a company: he was always squeezed between the boss (above) and junior staff (below), but was actually filling a key role for the company by linking the different parts together. The assumption was that, if father's position in the whole system were properly clarified, the parents and Aya would be able to secure their boundary as a nuclear family without cutting off connectedness with the extended family.

This kind of problem around in-law conflicts is common among Japanese families when three generations share the same household or live close by. The solution to these entangled relationships in the extended family is to provide a more comfortable balance between all parties and their competing needs, rather than cutting off certain relationships in order to secure others. A problem is likely to arise as the result of differences in values among the family members about what the balance should be. A husband may emphasize the relationship with his parents more than his wife does, while his wife may emphasize the spousal relationship more than he does. The favorable solution is to secure both relationships without cutting off either of them. From our clinical experience, dysfunctional families tend to have less coalition between the couple and more between the generations. It may be a safe option to underscore the generational Souvndary as in Britain, because the fact that the family has sought help from a third-party professional rather than within their kinship network already indicates that their traditional style of the family structure, which emphasizes the hierarchical line, is crumbling and requires a review of their problem-solving capacities for boundary setting and distance regulation.

Dilemmas in Therapy

The next family illustrates the major dilemmas that Japanese families and therapists face in family therapy practice, that is, the expected role of the therapist and the difficulties for the families in attending therapy sessions.

Case 3. Naomi, a Japanese girl of 16, came to England 3 years before with her family because of her father's job assignment. Her family consisted of parents in their 40s, an elder brother, an elder sister, and Naomi as the youngest. Naomi became extremely Angry and violent with her parents over her difficulty with school work. She became agitated late at night. She would wake up her parents and blame them for putting her in such an impossible position by coming to England.

Her parents, who were highly educated, laid great emphasis on hard work and academic achievement for their children. There was a shared belief in the family that her brother and sister were bright enough to respond to the parents' expectations. Although the parents recognized Naomi's talent in art and music, which were not counted as academic subjects, she had been labeled as lazy and less bright.

One of the issues the Japanese author tried to explore in the session, as suggested by the team of British therapists, was attempted past solutions. He tried to be neutral and t asked, in the form of circular questions, how they had managed Naomi and other children, t given the difficulties they were facing as 4 parents. Mother refused to answer his question. She was expecting his professional expertise to be expressed in the form of a direct and authoritative solution to the problem of how they should deal with Naomi when she was l agitated. She was not expecting him to ask all 1 these questions, which she considered irrelevant.

Father, on the other hand, was trying to be polite and to show his respect for the role of the therapist. He was very apologetic about his wife's impolite attitudes toward the therapist, and addressed him as "doctor" at the beginning or end of every statement. The father said they had tried everything but nothing had worked, and their problem was so immediate and serious that they expected "Doctor Tamura's personal advice or guidance!"

The parents in this case expected the therapist to be personal and directive. They expected Tamura, as a therapist, to be a part of the system, presumably as an authoritative and knowledgeable figure, and to solve the problem on their behalf. They were also trying to be polite to the therapist. This attitude indicated their view of the therapist as an authority figure who would direct them in the right way.

The expected role of the therapist varies by cultures (Jenkins, 1990). The basic assumption in Britain is that, although a therapist and a family may form a therapeutic system in the sessions, family and therapist are separate and individual entities. A therapist is basically regarded as a third-party agent who would work as a facilitator to enable the family to solve their own problem through the use of their own resources.

Japanese clients expect the therapist to be authoritative, directive, and closely connected. They may wish to regard the therapist as a family member (Ho, 1987) who takes on a parental role. In order to be credible, therapists must be old enough and socially well-respected. They are usually called *sensei*, a respected title widely used for teachers, doctors, lawyers, and members of the Diet.

By saying "We failed everything, so we need your immediate help!" they showed they were in a state of crisis, and felt totally incompetent. Munakata (1986) has described this as typical of Japanese patients who seek the therapist's indulgence and expect to be in a dependency relationship. Unless this emotional exchange occurs, they feel anxious, dissatisfied, and disorientated. The families depend on the therapist and they have to feel assured that they are accepted and cared for. This desire is close to the concept of *amae* (Doi, 1973), the desire to be the passive recipient of love. Patients may deliberately act childishly to convey their wish to be dependent.

There are a number of reasons why Japanese families are generally unwilling to see family therapists. First, they usually present their problems with tremendous sense of failure. A cultural pattern provides explanations of health and illness, definitions of normality and deviance, and guidelines for how to be acceptably deviant within the given culture (Lau, 1990). Physical illness is the only form of deviance that is socially permissible in Japan (Munakata, 1986). Psychological and behavioral problems are viewed as a lack of willpower or self-control.

Second, for families to have to tank about their personal problems to somebody outside of their kinship networks brings a deep sense of shame. Japanese make a fine distinction between what is inside and what is outside of the support network (Doi, 1985). Any emotion and problems are shared within what they perceive as inside, but it brings a sense of shame if one has to talk about an inside issue to somebody outside. Such behaviors as school refusal or alcohol dependence are not considered problems that call for the involvement of third-party experts; they are private problems that families are expected to control and take responsibility for. It is only when the family becomes completely exhausted that psychotherapy may be sought. By the time the family comes for therapy, therefore, they are often overwhelmed by a sense of crisis.

Third, some of the family members may be convinced that they need therapy, but others may not and refuse to attend the session. It is often mothers who first seek help for their children's problems. Even if the therapist asks them to come with their husbands to the session, they often are not successful because their husbands still deny the need of professional help. Fathers are usually the last ones to be motivated for family sessions. Many Japanese therapists regard this as the major hindrance to implementing family therapy in the Japanese context. There are two reasons for the difficulty over fathers' involvement: their peripheral position in the family and their commitment to work. It is often the case in the traditional family that mother and children are closely attached, and father peripheral to them. It is supposed to be mother's job to take care of their children, and the child's problem is seen as her responsibility. A mother is the one who should accompany her child for treatment, but not father. The reluctant father may say he is too busy to take a half day off to attend the family session. The task of motivating fathers is often painstaking and difficult, but, once engaged, they will usually manage to attend despite the earlier excuses of not knowing how to be involved with domestic matters.

Fourth, families are very reluctant to express themselves openly in conjoint family sessions. A mother may be able to complain about her husband at an individual session, but would not do so in a session where her husband and children are present. There are two reasons for this. One is the value placed on covert communication style, which discourages direct confrontation or criticism of others. The other reason is the hierarchical nature of the family structure. A wife cannot directly criticize her husband because of her complementary position. A father may find it difficult to share his feelings in front of his wife and children because he feels that he needs to maintain his detached and authoritative position in the family.

There are various strategies to counteract these difficulties. The joining process is crucial for Japanese family because they feel vulnerable and powerless when they have to present problems to the therapist. It is important to assess the family's expectation of the therapist. The therapist should accept, confirm, and support the family's worldview, and should try to feel the family members' pain in order to engage them at the initial stage of therapy (Minuchin, 1974). The family needs to gain a sense of connectedness to the therapist so that it can form a secure system wherein all problems and emotions can be safely shared and explored. Unless the therapist wins the family's trust so that the therapist is included inside of it, family members will be reluctant to share their real feelings.

The structural model may fit well for families that expect the therapists to be authoritative and directive (DiNicola, 1985; Jung, 1984). This does not necessarily mean being directive in the sense of imposing the therapist's definition of normality, but, rather, being assertive and active in the session so that the family can see that the therapist is a capable sensei (teacher). At the same time, the therapist always needs to be cautious about becoming too close and connected to the family, which would reduce the therapist's activity and deprive the family of their self-healing potential. The therapist may need to maintain a delicate balance between allowing the family to feel connected, and yet creating space between them to avoid excessive dependency.

A matchmaker of the arranged marriage holds a crucial role mediating any problem in an arranged marriage, and used to be the only accepted third party allowed entry into the internal affairs of a family. Family therapy would gain in popularity if therapists adopt some of the techniques of the matchmakers. They usually meet each prospective partner and their families separately, before and after the conjoint meeting. Crucial issues are discussed at meetings with only one side being involved. The conjoint meeting is more or less a formality. Bearing systemic thinking in mind, a therapist can use individual sessions in different ways. A therapist may choose to see individual members only before the conjoint session in order to engage them, or may use individual sessions more frequently in between the conjoint family sessions. Individual sessions have some advantages for Japanese families. It confirms their communication style, which avoids direct confrontations. It is particularly useful when trying to engage unmotivated fathers who are reluctant to come to a conjoint session. The father can lie asked to come as a "link therapist" (Landau, 1982) so that his authoritative position in the family is not challenged.

Mode of Psychotherapy

Verbal communication has always been a main vehicle for change in the tradition of Western psychotherapy. It is widely accepted that new meanings are created through therapeutic conversation (Anderson & Goolishian, 1988).

A British couple sought therapy for their children, ages 10 and 11, whose behaviors at school had deteriorated after their parents had divorced. At the first therapy session, mother said that her children should see a therapist on their own so that they could express their feelings, that she herself got over the trauma of the divorce by talking to many people on various occasions. "The more you talk about the problem, the more you will get a different angle and feel better."

Mother's belief in talking through as a solution is commonly shared in Britain. After bringing unresolved emotions into the open, that is, making the unconscious conscious, one should be able to manage these feelings, because they have been differentiated from an individual's self. A person can more effectively deal with problems by externalizing them (Tomm, 1989), which is a widely accepted way of solving problems in Britain. Psychodynamic theory can be thought of as a process of externalizing by making the unconscious conscious.

The Japanese traditional solution has been not to externalize but to internalize, which is a way of maintaining an integrated whole. Tomm has described this as "inner externalization" (Tomm, Suzuki, & Suzuki, 1990). Nonverbal techniques have been the main vehicle/ of Japanese traditional therapies. The traditional Japanese psychotherapies, namely Morita, Naikan, and Zen, cause the client to spend some time in silence and isolation, and to look into his or her own thoughts (Reynolds, 1980). Their underlying theory about change is influenced by Buddhism. When one manages to cut off all the outside noise and influences, one can hear one's true voice, which is innately good. A Japanese philosopher psychiatrist, Morita, at the turn of the century, applied Buddhist thinking in the treatment of his neurotic patients; this later developed into Morita therapy, one of the most popular, indigenous models of psychotherapy in Japan. According to Morita therapy,

> there is no neurotic person as such, only a mind that is more or less blocked from its natural flow at some given point in time. We are all victims of blocking at one time or another. A person we label neurotic in comparison with the rest of us simply blocks more frequently, more strongly, or in response to some unusual situations. We are all more or less neurotic—if you want to use that term— different only in degree, not in kind. The goal of therapy is to so immerse the patient in the needs of the moment that he loses awareness of the symptom, the nagging anxiety, the unappealable pain. If he sits and ruminates on it, he only exaggerates the problem and inflates its effect on his consciousness. (Reynolds, 1980, p. 14)

Meditation is traditionally used as a means of internalizing a problem. It is believed that one feels pain, bereavement, or worries only because one tries to struggle against the flow of nature. By sitting silently and eliminating all the outside "noise," one becomes in touch with the true self, which is intrinsically connected with the mother nature, able to accept the self and the pain because one is not an isolated existence but a part of the total wholeness. Meditation-and the use of silence are the keys to devising a Japanese model of family therapy.

Although emphasis is shifting to the process of interviewing itself (Tomm, 1987), the final intervention may still be indispensable to maximize the therapeutic impact. As seen in Case 3, family members may expect to be cured by complying with the therapist's directives, but not by the therapeutic debate itself. They may be frustrated if the therapist only asks questions and gives no advice.

Nonverbal techniques like sculpting and conjoint family drawing have been widely used among Japanese therapists. The use of a genogram of at least three generations is crucial in understanding the family. It is useful not only for eliciting transgenerational patterns and family myths, but also for illustrating the whole picture of the family system. Even if the family consists of a two generational household and the extended family lives miles away, they would still maintain close emotional links and expect to be involved in important issues.

Conclusion

In our view, the Japanese family therapy scene is reaching the second stage. The task of the first stage in the 1980s was mainly concerned with "importing" systemic thinking and Western schools of family therapy. The task of therapists in 19908 is to develop a model that is congruent with Japanese values and family processes. In doing so, we need to begin by clarifying the differences between our culture and the Western European culture (see Figure 1).

Systemic thinking, the basic premise of Western models of family therapy, which deals with the pattern of relationships, is applicable to Japanese families only when therapists are aware of their own cultural value system that emphasizes the connectedness of relationships. They also need to be reminded that this value orientation sets the reality of family lives in a way that may be quite different from those in other cultures. In particular, the following areas need to be taken into account in order that Japanese therapists can maximize their therapeutic effects. When working with the structural model, they need to assess what the "functional" family structure is, and be careful not to impose blindly the Western values of an egalitarian, nuclear family. They should also be aware that strategies aiming at therapeutic impact through verbal interaction are built on premises that emphasize verbal communication. Strategies that emphasize the nonverbal mode of communication may show a better fit with Japanese families.

The way in which the problem is understood and the desired direction for change are also colored by the cultural belief system. We have discussed the process of integration as the direction to pursue in Japan, which can be contrasted with the process of differentiation in Britain. But, from the universalist point of view, both the pro-

cesses of differentiation and integration are equally necessary ingre-
dients for human growth in any culture. Japanese seem to overemphasize the process of integration and pay less attention to the process
of differentiation. Problems are often perceived by the Japanese therapists as the result of insufficient integration, for example, not enough
mother–child interdependence in early childhood. So therapy seems
to focus on how to facilitate functional integration through sensitivity to others and enhancement of the support network system. Exploring cultural differences would remind Japanese therapists of the
importance of differentiation. Now the direction of change for the
Japanese family would be to move from a foundation of family connectedness toward the process of integration of the whole system,
including respect for individual freedom and differentiation.

British values, by contrast, seem to overemphasize the importance of differentiation. Can recognition of Japanese values demonstrate to families of the Western world how people can be
effectively integrated within family systems?

References

Anderson, H., & Goolishian, H. A. (1988). Human systems as linguistic
  systems: Preliminary and evolving ideas about the implicator's for clinical
  theory. *Family Process, 27*, 371–393.
Bell, L. (1989). Song without words. *Family Therapy Networker, 13*(2),
  48–53.
Bott, D., & Hodes, M. (1989). Structural therapy for a West African family.
  Journal of Family Therapy, 11, 169–179.
Bowen, M. (1978). *Family therapy in clinical practice.* New York: Jason
  Aronson.
Brown, G. W., Monch, E. M., Carstairs, G. M., & Wing, J. K. (1962). Influ-
  ence of family life on the cource of schizophrenic illness. *British Jour-
  nal of Preventive and Social Medicine, 16*, 56–68.
Capra, F. (1975). *The Tao of physics.* London: Fontana.
Capra, F. (1982). *The turning point.* London: Fontana.
Colman, C. (1986). International family therapy: A view from Photo, Ja-
  pån. *Family Process, 25*, 651–664.
Cronen, V. E., Johnson, K. M., & Lannamann, J. W. (1982). Paradoxes, double
  binds, and reflexive loops: An alternative theoretics perspective. *Fam-
  ily Process, 21*, 91–112.
DiNicola, V. F. (1985). Family therapy and transcultural psychiatry: An
  emerging synthesis. *Transcultural Psychiatric Research Review, 22*(2),
  81–113; *22*(3), 151–180.
Doi, L. T. (1973). *The anatomy of dependence* (J. Beater, Trans.). Tokyo:
  Kodansha International.

Doi, L. T. (1985). *The anatomy of self: The individual versus society*, M. A. Harbison, Trans.). Tokyo: Kodansha International.

Falicov, C. J. (Ed.). (1983). *Cultural perspectives in family therapy*. Rockville, MD: Aspen.

Furnham, A., & Bochner, S. (1986). *Culture shock: Psychological reactions to unfamiliar environments*. London: Routledge & Kegan Paul.

Hall, E. T., & Hall, M. R. (1987). *Hidden differences: Doing business with the Japanese*. New York: Anchor Press.

Ho, M. K. (1987). *Family therapy with ethnic minorities*. Newbury Park, CA: Sage.

Hodes, M. (1985). Family therapy and the problem of cultural relativism: A reply to Dr. Lau. *Journal of Family Therapy*, *7*, 261–272.

Hodes, M. (1989). Annotation: Culture and family therapy. *Journal of Family Therapy*, *11*, 117–128

Hoffman, L. (1981). *Foundations of family therapy: A conceptual framework for systems change*. New York: Basic Books.

Hong, G. K. (1989). Application of cultural and environmental issues in family therapy with immigrant Chinese Americans. *Journal of Strategic and Systemic Therapies*, *8*, 14–21.

Jenkins, H. (1990). Csalad therapia: Family therapy training in Hungary. *Association for Child Psychology and Psychiatry Newsletter*, *12*(6), 9–13.

Johnson, F. A., Marsella, A. J., & Johnson, C. L. (1974). Social and psychological aspects of verbal behavior in Japanese-Americans. *American Journal of Psychiatry*, *131*, 580–583.

Jung, M. (1984). Structural family therapy: Its application to Chinese families. *Family Process*, *23*, 365–374.

Kamiko, T., & Masuda, K. (Eds.). (1981). *Family relationships of the Japanese: A cross-national comparison*. Tokyo: Yuhikaku.

Kawai, H. (1986). Violence in the home: Conflict between two principles—Maternal and paternal (pp. 297–306). In T. Lebra & W. Lebra (Eds.), *Japanese culture and behavior*. Honolulu: University of Hawaii Press.

Keeney, B. P. (1983). *Aesthetics of change*. New York: Guilford Press.

Kinzie, D., Sushaman, P. C., & Lee, M. (1972). Cross cultural family therapy—A Malaysian experience. *Family Process*, *11*, 59–67.

Landau, J. (1982). Therapy with families in cultural transition. In M. McGoldrick, J. K. Pearce, & J. Giordano (Eds.), *Ethnicity and family therapy* (pp. 552–572). New York: Guilford Press.

Lau, A. (1984). Transcultural issues in family therapy. *Journal of Family Therapy*, *6*, 91–112.

Lau, A. (1985). Cultural relativism—Relative agreement. *Journal of Family Therapy*, *7*, 273–275.

Lau, A. (1986). Family therapy across cultures. In J. L. Cox (Ed.), *Transcultural psychiatry* (pp. 234–252). London: Croom Helm.

Lau, A. (1988). Family therapy and ethnic minorities. In E. Street & W. Dryden (Eds.), *Family therapy in Britain* (pp. 234–252). Milton Keynes, England: Open University Press.

Lau, A. (1990). Psychological problems in adolescents from ethnic minorities. *British Journal of Hospital Medicine, 44*, 201–205.

Lewis, J. M., Beavers, W. R., Gossett, J. T., & Phillips, V. A. (1976). *No single thread: Psychological health in family systems.* New York: Brunner/Mazel.

Lock, M. (1986). Plea for acceptance: School refusal syndrome in Japan. *Social Science and Medicine, 23*(2), 99–112.

Long, S. O. (1987). *Family change and the life course in Japan.* Ithaca, NY: Cornell University East Asia Papers.

McGill, D. (1987). Language, cultural psychology, and family therapy: Japanese examples from an international perspective. *Contemporary Family Therapy, 9*, 283–293.

McGill, D., & Pearce, J. K. (1982). British families. In M. McGoldrick, J. K. Pearce, & J. Giordano (Eds.), *Ethnicity and family therapy* (pp. 457–479). New York: Guilford Press.

McGoldrick, M. (1982). Ethnicity and family therapy: An overview. In M. McGoldrick, J. K Pearce, & J. Giordano (Eds.), *Ethnicity and family therapy* (pp. 3–30). New York: Guilford Press.

McGoldrick, M. (1989a). Ethnicity and the family life cycle. In B. Carter & M. McGoldrick (Eds.), *The changing family life cycle: A framework for family therapy* (pp. 69–90). Boston: Allyn & Bacon.

McGoldrick, M. (1989b). The joining of families through marriage: The new couple. In B. Carter & M. McGoldrick (Eds.), *The changing family life cycle: A framework for family therapy* (pp. 209–233). Boston: Allyn & Bacon.

McGoldrick, M., & Preto, N. G. (1984). Ethnic intermarriage: Implications for therapy. *Family Process, 23*, 347–364.

Minuchin, S. (1974). *Families & family therapy.* Cambridge, MA: Harvard University Press.

Munakata, T. (1986). Japanese attitudes toward mental health and mental health care. In T. S. Lebra & W. P. Lebra (Eds.), *Japanese culture and behavior: Selected readings* (pp. 369–478). Honolulu: University of Hawaii Press.

Nagashima, N. (1973). A reversed world: Or is it? The Japanese way of communication and their attitudes towards alien cultures. In R. Horton & K. Finnegan (Eds.), *Modes of thought: Essays on thinking in Western and Non-Western societies* (pp. 92–111). London: Faber & Faber.

Papp, P. (1983). *The process of change.* New York: Guilford Press.

Reynolds, D. K. (1980). *The quiet therapies: Japanese pathways to personal growth.* Honolulu: University of Hawaii Press.

Roland, A. (1988). *In search of self in India and Japan: Toward a cross-cultural psychology.* Princeton, NJ: Princeton University Press.

Shon, S. P., & Ja, D. Y. (1982). Asian families. In M. McGoldrick, J. K. Pearce, & J. Giordano (Eds.), *Ethnicity and family therapy* (pp.208–228). New York: Guilford Press.

Skynner, R. (1987). Frameworks for viewing the family as a system. In A. Bentovim, G. G. Barnes, & A. Cooklin (Eds.), *Family therapy: Complementary frameworks of theory and practice* (Vol. 1, pp. 3–35). London: Academic Press.

Sluzki, C. E. (1979). Migration and family conflict. *Family Process, 18,* 379–390.

Tamura, T. (1990). Japan and family therapy. *Bulletin of the International Family Therapy Association, 3*(1), 6–7.

Tomm, K. (1987). Interventive interviewing: Part II. Reflexive questioning as a means to enable self-healing. *Family Process, 26,* 167–183.

Tomm, K. (1989). Externalizing the problem and internalizing personal agency. *Journal of Strategic and Systemic Therapies, 8*(1), 54–59.

Tomm, K., Suzuki, K., & Suzuki, K. (1990). The *kan-no-mushi*: An inner externalization that enables compromise? *Australian and New Zealand Journal of Family Therapy, 11,* 104–107.

Vaughn, C. E., & Leff, J. P. (1976). The influence of family and social factors on the course of psychiatric illness: A comparison of schizophrenic and depressed neurotic patients. *British Journal of Psychiatry, 129,* 125–137.

Vogel, E. (1967). The go-between in a developing society: The case of the Japanese marriage arranger. *Human Organization, 20,* 112–120.

Watanabe, M. (1974). The conception of nature in Japanese culture. *Science, 183,* 279–282.

Watts, A. W. (1961). *Psychotherapy East and West.* Harmondsworth, Middlesex, England: Penguin Books.

■ ■ ■

9

Using Solution-Focused Therapy With Korean Families

Sung Ja Song, PhD

Korea has nearly 5,000 years of history with its own language, culture, and traditions. Buddhism and Confucianism have played an important historical role in the early cultural heritage of Korea (Choi, 1994). Koreans' strong commitment to family is rooted in the core concepts from Buddhism and Confucianism (K. T. Lee, 1983). At the end of the 20th century, Korea has been undergoing remarkable social and cultural changes in the course of modernization, swift industrialization, and economic growth.

Koreans have been fighting Western influences because it is difficult for them to discard their traditional customs, thought patterns, and habits derived from the 2,000-year-old Confucian tradition (Hyun, 1995). A recent study conducted on values in five cities in Korea found that housewives still hold very strongly to all of the traditional Korean values (Song, 1995b).

Korean Cultural Values and Family Structure

Valuing Family Relationships

The fundamental principle governing relationships among individuals, family, and community is best articulated in the "five cardinal relations." Some of these relations are based on the family, the state, and the community. Virtues such as responsibility, wisdom, benevolence, obedience, loyalty, filial piety, and respect are essential to the five cardinal relations principles (U. Kim, 1991). The core emphases within the relations are hierarchical, with the major guiding principle of "reciprocity." To ensure harmony and order in the family and to further these five cardinal relations in society, Koreans abided by the cardinal value of filial piety. In Confucian thought, everybody observes the fundamental principle consisting of harmonious and peaceful social order (Hyun, 1995) and the family is considered the prototype for all relationships (U. Kim, 1991; C. H. Lee, 1990).

The importance of the family in Korean culture has been confirmed by a study done on the psychological connotations of "self" with a sample of Korean and American male participants. According to these researchers (Maday & Szalay, 1976), Korean respondents' verbal associations to the concept of "me" converged to follow five important themes in descending order: (a) family, and love; (b) ideals, happiness, and freedom; (c) hope, ambition, and success; (d) money, material, and goods; and (e) education, knowledge, and intelligence. In contrast, American responses showed a convergence around the individual's physical and emotional conditions. The five most frequent themes of concern were in the following order: (a) I, person, individual; (b) other people; (c) tiredness, loneliness, and physical appearance; (d) being good, friendly, and sociable; and (e) family, and love.

These findings noted that the American conception of "me" focused on the individual self and that it was detached from kin affiliation and surrounded by strangers. The Korean concept of "me," on the other hand, included family members (e.g., father, mother, brother, and sister) as a major constituent of the self.

Family Structure

In traditional Korean families, marriages were arranged by the parents or grandparents to ensure the family's prosperity and propagation of the husband's family. The dominant relationship is still more likely to be placed on the parent–child dyad rather than the husband–wife dyad. The emphasis on hierarchies by gender, generation, age, and class is very much a part of the Korean society. Although on the surface the emphasis on hierarchy structure seems to have gone through some changes, underneath it still remains very much of the Korean thinking (B. L. Kim, 1996). The traditional values regarding the relationships between parent–child and husband–wife dyads continue to remain firm. Parents are to support and guide, and children are to respect and obey, regardless of their own opinion.

Although families are becoming smaller in size, the strong tradition of the extended family endures. For example, when a couple gets married, the husband and his in-laws are likely to be involved in the decision-making process within that marriage (e.g., how many children the couple will have). Though family structure is gradually changing in modern Korea, the values and characteristics continue to be traditional.

Parent–Child Relationship

In Confucian cultures, mothers and fathers have different roles. The father is the symbolic head of the family, and the mother is the major caretaker. The traditional role of a mother is to nurture and provide support, and the father's role is to discipline and to provide financial support within the traditional model of the Korean family. The parental role tends to be complementary rather than symmetrical. The boundary between them is enmeshed, and the focus is to meet all of the children's needs, particularly those of the first child. It is common for mothers to be overprotective and to interfere in raising and disciplining their sons. After the son is married, the mother-in-law "meddles" in her son's marriage, including the everyday activities. Most Korean mothers-in-law think of meddling as their duty, born of love and concern. Usually parents-in-law help raise the grandchildren and provide emotional support as well (Berg & Jaya, 1993). This type of socialization creates a strong bond of interdependence.

Devotion is an important element in both the mother–child and the father–child relationship. In a mother–child relationship, the devotion is complemented with indulgence, and in the father–child relationship devotion is complemented by strictness. Children display their devotion to their father by being obedient, respectful, and compliant (U. Kim, 1991). The devotion shown by a mother to her children serves as a foundation and a model for the children's devotion to their father. The respective roles of a father and a mother are best summarized in a popular Chinese and Korean phrase, "strict father, benevolent mother."

Usually, the parents would financially support the children when necessary. When the parents grow old and become financially and physically needy, the children are obligated to care for their parents. This implies that parent–child relationships are very close and mutually reciprocal. In this way, parents and children exchange the role of caretaker.

Communication Patterns of Koreans

In Korean culture, the attitude toward open and free expression of thoughts and feelings is different from the West. Because harmonious interpersonal relationships are so highly valued in Korea culture, direct confrontation, which may lead to disagreement, confrontation, and loss, is avoided whenever possible. Therefore, much of the communication style is indirect, with the goal of talking around the point (Song, 1995a). On the other hand, Western society values the ability to express ideas and feelings openly. Individuals are encouraged to speak out, tell it like it is, and openness is highly valued. Verbal openness and expressiveness are certainly one of the desirable attributes of the so-called "good therapy candidate" (Shon & Ja, 1982). Song (1995b) found that when couples experience conflict, indirect, rather than direct, communication is usually used in their attempts to solve problems.

Negotiation Through Mediation

Korea has a long tradition of solving problems through negotiation and mediation, rather than direct confrontation (Berg & Jaya, 1993; B. L. Kim, 1996; E. Lee, 1996). All negotiations, including family matters, marital conflicts, and contracts (whether business or personal) are carried out through mediators. Traditionally, mediators are chosen for their fairness and wisdom. This works well as long as there was respect for the mediator's authority.

Throughout the life cycle of Koreans, different people play the role of mediators, depending on the developmental phase and the situation. For example, children in Korean families are told constantly that younger siblings are to respect and obey older siblings and older siblings are to yield to and care for younger siblings. When conflicts between siblings occur, one of the parents usually plays the role of a mediator, administering punishment accordingly (B. L. Kim, 1996). Teachers also serve as mediators for children. Students are expected to respect teachers, and thus students tend to listen and accept the teacher's opinion readily.

In Korea, there may be different mediators for different situations. Mediators and family therapists are in a particularly good position to mediate family conflicts because of their positions of authority. The therapist may find it more productive to meet with the parties in conflict separately before bringing the family members together. Expecting them to air their differences at the outset is too confrontational and will not enhance peaceful negotiation.

Whether the conflict is between parent and child, husband and wife, or other combinations of family members, it is usually more productive to see them individually first, listen to each view, and then make suggestions to diffuse the tension and encourage negotiation (Berg & Jaya, 1993).

Treatment Considerations

Traditional Western psychotherapeutic approaches are based on the assumptions of individuation, independence, self-disclosure, and verbal expression of feelings (E. Lee, 1996; Tseng & Hsu, 1991). Long-term insight-oriented therapy may be antithetical to Korean values, which emphasize harmonious relationships, interdependence, self-control, repression of emotions, and short-term, result-oriented solutions (C. H. Lee, 1990). For Koreans, solution-focused, short-term therapy seems to be more effective than traditional Western psychotherapy (Chung, 1995; Huh, 1995; E. Lee, 1996). This section briefly describes three major issues related to providing therapy to Korean families. These issues include client's expectations, assessment of family readiness for therapy, and family problems.

Clients' Expectations: Pragmatic Solutions and Positive Reframing

Most families seek therapy during a family crisis. They are already very anxious, defensive, and deeply shamed about seeking help because it implies a loss of face. They do not anticipate receiving understanding or help with their problems and often assume that the therapist will be critical, punitive, and authoritative (B. L. Kim, 1996). Nevertheless, the clients' expectation of being able to solve problems by themselves is low. Therefore, the clients tend to depend on the therapist or the mediator to solve their problems. This is due to their lack of experience with conflict management.

Commonly, Korean couples tend to see the problems as a matter of right or wrong and expect the therapist to resolve them by proving their partner wrong. Men also tend to invoke male superiority to win their point. Usually, a wife brings the case to a nonfamily member instead of talking directly to her husband to avoid confrontation with him. The women often practice patience and suppress their emotions (Song, 1995a).

Koreans who seek therapy initially complaining of physical or behavioral problems expect immediate and specific solutions to their problems. Once the clients perceive the therapist's role, they tend to gradually trust and accept the therapist. Then the clients can commit to therapy and often become very open with their feelings and opinions (S. C. Kim, 1985).

For Koreans, face-saving and concern about others' evaluations are particularly important. Therefore, a therapist's positive reframing, along with compliments, works well with Korean families—this method avoids shaming clients while preserving their dignity and proper roles in the family.

Family Readiness and Involvement in Therapy

Koreans seldom seek professional help. Sometimes, they consider the emotional pain and worry caused by relational or environmental problems as immutable destiny, needing to be endured without complaints. They usually do not see individual problems as family related. They rarely agree with the suggestion that the problem is the group's instead of the identified client's (E. Lee, 1996). Many Koreans seek help from mental health or family therapy professionals only as the last resort after they have exhausted all other resources. They usually come in for help in a state of crisis with the expectation of an immediate "cure" (E. Lee, 1996). They expect a quick diagnosis and do not understand the purpose of lengthy evaluation and the apparent lack of visible treatment in the initial process.

Because of the traditional hierarchy, face-saving (*che-myun*), and shame, it is very difficult for the clients to express thoughts and negative feelings verbally and openly. Generally, Korean husbands or fathers are quite resistant to attending family sessions or allowing the therapist to enter into the family system. The admission of emotional problems and acceptance of help from outside the family network may be interpreted as a sign of weakness and losing face for many traditional Korean men. In the event that their children are in trouble and the parents are forced to receive treatment, they usually send their wives as family representatives to deal with service agencies.

Many young fathers participate in family therapy for their children because they value the obligation and responsibility of the parent's role. But husbands usually do not participate in family therapy if it is for a marital problem. Furthermore, for parents to discuss their "adult" problems or to express their sadness in front of the children is considered inappropriate because it suggests a loss of face and paternal authority.

A flexible subfamily system approach in the establishment of therapeutic relationships with family members at the beginning phase can be very helpful. For example, an effective method is for a clinician to interview the parents first, then the identified client, and then the siblings. This allows the parents to discuss their adult concerns and express their emotions freely in the absence of the children and the children to negotiate issues they may not be comfortable discussing when their parents are present (E. Lee, 1996).

Common Korean Family Problems

On the basis of statistics from family therapy literature and other research materials (Song, 1995b), some of the most common family problems are husbands' affairs outside the marriage, financial difficulties, differences in personalities, and problems with children. Rather than seeking solutions through discussions as equal partners, husbands tend to demand obedience from their wives. This sometimes escalates into uncontrollable confrontation and violence. This may be explained by the traditional expectation of the dominance of man over woman and by men's fear of women's status being rapidly changed to become more independent and outspoken.

There has been an increase in the demand for therapy on issues related to children. This is a change from the past, when parents were closed minded with regard to child-related issues. The most common issues brought into therapy in Korea relate to academic performance and college admission. Korean parents' high expectations and demands of their children are perceived to be the main causal factor for such issues.

Another ongoing issue in Korean families is conflict with in-laws. Although the family structure is shifting from the extended family to the nuclear family, parents are still very much interested in their children's affairs. Children also feel the obligation to express care and concern to their parents, whether they are living together or not. These unstated expectations of parents and children often produce conflict in the family.

Strategies and Skills

Solution-focused therapy is a strengths-based therapy model developed at the Brief Family Therapy Center in Milwaukee, Wisconsin, by Steve de Shazer, Insoo Kim Berg, and associates over the past 15 years. This model is being applied to a wide variety of clinical work, such as inpatient psychiatric disorders, alcohol abuse, school-related behavior problems, and spouse abuse. Critics of the solution-focused approach have challenged its simplicity, brevity, and the credibility of its outcome claims (Nichols & Schwartz, 1995). At times, the approach has been portrayed modestly—as a way to start therapy on a positive note, with the option to switch to other methods if the problem perseveres (de Shazer, 1988). Such claims raise the concern that, in some cases, the therapist's need for clients to think positively may induce denial or minimizing of problems.

Strategies of the solution-focused therapist include (a) tracking solution behaviors, (b) increasing motivation toward a new set of behaviors by reinforcing times when the problem is absent and constantly complimenting and attending to small differences in behavioral change, (c) taking a client-centered orientation in which the therapist starts from the cognitive frame of the client and works with him or her to construct solutions that will help accomplish goals, (d) focusing on the future instead of the present or the past, and (e) using presuppositional language aimed at helping clients restructure cognitive meanings about themselves and their problems.

Solution-focused therapists often use questioning techniques, such as (a) exception questions, (b) relationship questions, (c) scaling questions, (d) coping and motivation questions, and (e) miracle questions (Berg, 1994; Berg & Miller, 1992b). Although solution-focused brief family therapy was developed in the U.S., it seems to offer a fit in the treatment of Korean families; however, adaptations are needed to make it more applicable to the Korean culture. Therefore, the skills and strategies of solution-focused brief family therapy that I have found effective, based on my experiences working with Korean families, are described below.

Developing Cooperation Between Therapist and Client. Koreans emphasize hierarchy and demonstrate respect for professionals, reflecting the fact that most Koreans are more comfortable in "top-down" structured relationships. Thus, as in other relationships, in a therapist–client relationship, the therapist is believed to be in a higher position because of his or her professional knowledge. This may lead clients to be dependent on the therapist. Such expectation stems from the thought that the person in the higher position is to take care of the person in the lower position. Paradoxically, this allows the therapist to be more effective. This "joining" by the therapist does help the client to be more cooperative and open (Berg, 1994; Berg & Miller, 1992b).

Coping Rather Than Changing the Problem. Koreans highly value harmonious relationships and therefore strive to cope with any stressful situations. For example, in most cases of marital conflict, only the wife comes for treatment. Usually, she complains about her husband's neglectful behavior and family abuse. She tries to describe her long-standing sacrifice for the family and how her husband is wrong and she is right. She never talks about divorcing him, however, because of her obligation to take care of the family and children. She doesn't expect that the problem will be solved; instead, she would like to cope with the difficult situation.

Clients feel most comfortable working to find solutions from the first session. They are determined to find ways to deal with their situations now, rather than in the past or in the future. This solution-focused approach emphasizes the transfer of focus from that of probing the causes and the complaints to what the client and the therapist can do to look for solutions to problems (de Shazer, 1988).

Reinforcing Successful Experiences. Traditional Korean culture is changing rapidly in many different ways as a result of modernization. Many different factors influence this change, such as sex, age, education, and geographical location (Hyun, 1995). In the process of the rapid transformation of the traditional culture, the cultural differences between social strata, social groups, and families are becoming more conspicuous. For example, when a married daughter comes home from a fight with her husband, some parents would lecture her to go back and work the problems out, but other parents would be on their daughter's side unconditionally. The former parents may serve as a helping resource in the couple's therapy, but the latter parents may become a hindrance. Therefore, it is important to assess the patterns of the family to avoid any unhelpful alliances.

Priority on Setting Goals. As mentioned earlier, Koreans are family oriented, valuing harmony and cooperation within the family. Moreover, through family and especially parents' validation, one confirms oneself and is strongly motivated to participate in society. Thus, the establishment and realization of individual-oriented goals would be difficult for Koreans. For example, when the goal is established on the basis of family orientation, families would be very cooperative in the process of accomplishment, making its achievement easier. It would be much easier for the therapist if the goal is set around the children or the parents of the couple rather than the couple themselves. This requires that major considerations be given to what the clients regard as most important (Berg & Miller, 1992a; de Shazer, 1991).

Meaning of Circumstances Being More Important Than the Content of the Problem. Koreans tend to focus more on the definition of the situation than the actual problem. For example, if the financial difficulties of the family are due to children's education expenses, the family is willing to pay for them at all cost. If a wife feels stress from taking care of her sick parent-in-law, her husband and other family members' validation of the sacrifices would encourage her to cope. Similarly, clients do value the therapist's compliments and validation or recognition of feelings, which allows for reframing and ascribing positive meaning to behaviors that are sometimes perceived as negative.

Using Face-Saving for Problem Solving: An Approach for Involuntary Clients. It is not an overstatement to call Korea a "face-saving" culture. Koreans are careful to take others into consideration throughout most decision-making processes. It is important to leave others with a good impression at all times. In the West, this is viewed as superficial. In Korea, to maintain saving face, it is necessary to try one's best to be trustworthy and to act respectfully to others. Because of this value, it is difficult for husbands or fathers to be involved in therapy. When they do participate, they are self-protective and cautious toward the therapist. An effective method to deal with such reluctance it to validate and compliment them on the accomplishment they have made as fathers and as husbands. Once this validation is given to the fathers or husbands, they can begin to trust the therapist and to be cooperative in solving problems (Berg, 1994; Berg & Miller, 1992b; de Shazer, 1988).

This is the technique that takes Korean culture into account and is used with clients who refuse to participate in, or are unreceptive to, the family therapy (Berg, 1994; Berg & Miller, 1992a). Compliments are given to the client in recognition of the efforts he has made to solve the problem and the successful experiences he has had in the past.

Systematic Involvement of a Family Using the Hierarchy System. As stated, harmonious relationships among family members are important, and thus family members avoid direct confrontations at all cost and abstain from aggravating any potential problems. Moreover, the difficulty of verbally expressing suppressed feelings and thoughts makes family members reluctant to come to sessions at the same time. In cases in which family members are present from the first session, individuals are not able to express themselves frankly, which tends to place blame on others. For example, if a therapist is not able to prevent or control conflicts between a couple, the husband may think he has lost face and the wife may think the therapy session is the cause of their problems. Thus, they are not likely to return to therapy.

Therapists must be flexible in treating individual members. It is important for the treatment to use the existing hierarchy of the family system, working with the system rather than trying to change the system. This emphasizes the flexibility of role performance and various interventions by the therapist. For example, a therapist may encourage clients to decide for themselves the frequency and the number of the family members involved in therapy (Berg, 1994; Berg & Jaya, 1993; de Shazer et al., 1986).

Changing Clients' Attitudes by Using Revised Scale Questions. Open boasting is a Korean cultural taboo. The culture values humility, and it is not deemed appropriate for men to express their positive feelings about their family openly. One way to appear humble is to put oneself down in front of others and to deny compliments made by others. In the meantime, Koreans do have respect for others' opinions, especially those of professionals. Therefore, throughout family therapy, it is important not only for the therapist, but also for the clients to affirm the changes being made in the process.

Although clients want changes to occur, they also have the potential to easily reject any changes or express negative viewpoints about the changes. These reactions may be surprising to beginning clinicians, but it should be understood as a way for clients to be humble. Also, in such situations, the use of tentative language is more effective because the Korean language is tentative compared with the declarative statements of the English language. It is critical for therapists to have some concrete tools or theories for clients to be able to view the changes occurring throughout the sessions. This process will enable clients to feel confident about the changes occurring and to be even more motivated to seek solutions.

It is the use of revised scale questions that helps clients decide on the operational objectives, plan the implementation schedule, and self-ascertain their progress (Berg, 1994; Berg & Jong, 1996; Berg & Miller, 1992a, 1992b).

Providing Therapeutic Messages and Tasks. The predominant educational approach does not encourage experimenting or being creative, either at home or at school. The children and students are expected to listen to and obey parents and teachers. The educational system deters Koreans from challenging authority and exercising creativity in finding solutions.

Generally, clients are used to receiving a diagnosis and being prescribed medicine. Therefore, they feel unsure about finding solutions through family therapy. At times, clients may demand a prescription for medicine or to see concrete and visible solutions. In such cases, it is effective for the therapist to give a brief assignment or task to the clients. Such a method will also motivate the clients to cooperate more with the therapist.

Suggestions for Treatment

Here are some ideas to be considered when using solution-focused therapy skills with Korean families.

1. Clients prefer an informal relationship in the working relationship. Because Koreans value interpersonal relationships highly, clients often expect to experience a more informal and close relationship with the therapist. For example, they want therapists to share personal information about their age, marital status, and significant others. This is to express concern and good feeling and is not intended to be intrusive or nosy. It is also important to accept the client's friendliness and not to misjudge the client's concern. Therefore, one can expect good results if one attempts from the beginning to form an informal relationship.

2. Clients want to ventilate suppressed emotion first. If a client is asked in the first session "What kind of help do you want through family therapy?" they may be perplexed. Clients generally have the need to express their emotion first, and only thereafter will they cooperate in the setting of treatment goals. Korean clients tend to equate the ventilation of frustration with the description of problems.

3. Koreans are not used to questions, but brief family therapy recommends useful questions. In their daily lives, Koreans are reluctant to express to others their thoughts and feelings or raise questions. Raising many questions to the person in the position of higher level in the hierarchy is not considered good manners. If a therapist raises too many questions, clients may feel uneasy and withdrawn. Questions that are simple and short seem to work the best; only then can positive responses be secured.

4. Koreans are not used to the exchange of compliments. Regardless of cultural background, we all need recognition and vali-

dation from others. Koreans, however, are not accustomed to showing any sign of recognition, even when someone deserves it. Instead, they are quick to criticize when someone commits certain errors. Therefore, for the Korean therapist, it is difficult to recognize and praise clients in the open. If the therapist expresses compliments, clients may think that the therapist considers the client an immature child and may become suspicious about the therapist's intention. It may reduce his or her confidence in the therapist. If used with adequate considerations of the clients' needs, however, then this technique definitely produces positive clinical results.

Conclusion

The Korean culture has been changing rapidly during the last generation. These changes vary according to the sex, age, level of education, and economic status of individuals. Many people are still very much family centered, maintaining mutually interdependent relationships in the family. At the same time, relationships outside the family tend to show individualistic and highly competitive orientations. Because of such differences in the culture of modern Korea, one cannot make sweeping generalizations. It is very important to understand the relationships between the problems of the client and the cultural backgrounds of his or her family in assessing problems, determining treatment goals, and selecting appropriate treatment strategies.

What one must remember in thinking about treating Koreans is, first of all, to understand the differences between the Western and Korean cultures. Second, recurrent training and supervision are necessary for the creative, adjusted application of existing theories to Korean families. Last, persistent experimental studies and scientific appraisal of results are needed for future development of family therapy suitable to the Koran culture.

References

Berg, I. (1994). *Family based services: A solution-focused approach.* New York: Norton.

Berg, I., & Jaya, A. (1993). Different and same: Family therapy with Asian-American families. *Journal of Marital and Family Therapy, 19* (1), 31–38.

Berg, I. K., & Jong, P. D. (1996). Solution-building conversations: Co-constructing a sense of competence with clients. *Families in Society: The Journal of Contemporary Human Services, 77*, 376–391.

Berg, I. K., & Miller, S. D. (1992a). Working with Asian American clients: One person at a time. *Families in Society: The Journal of Contemporary Human Services, 73*, 356–363

Berg, I. K., & Miller, S. D. (1992b). *Working with the problem drinker.* New York: Norton.

Choi, B. Y. (1994). *Koreans' social character.* Seoul, Korea: Neuti Namoo.

Chung, M. J. (1995). A conversation analysis of solution-focused family therapy sessions. *Korean Journal of Family Therapy, 3*, 1–20.

de Shazer, S. (1988). *Clues: Investigating solutions in brief therapy.* New York: Norton.

de Shazer, S. (1991). *Putting differences to work.* New York: Norton.

de Shazer, S., Berg, I. K., Lipchik, E., Nunnally, E., Molnar, A., & Weiner-Davis, M. (1986). Brief therapy: Focused solution development. *Family Process, 25*, 207–221.

Huh, N. S. (1995). A solution focused brief family therapy with spouse abuse. *Korean Journal of Family Therapy, 3*, 30–35.

Hyun, K. (1995). *Culture and the self: Implications for Koreans' mental health.* Unpublished doctoral dissertation, University of Michigan.

Kim, B. L. (1996). Korean families. In M. McGoldrick, J. Giordano, & J. Pearce (Eds.), *Ethnicity and family therapy* (pp. 281–294). New York: Guilford Press.

Kim S. C. (1985). Family therapy for Asian Americans: A strategic–structural frame work. *Psychotherapy, 22*, 342–348.

Kim, U. (1991). *Introduction to individualism and collectivism: Social and applied issues.* Unpublished manuscript, University of Hawaii.

Lee, C. H. (1990, June). *Comparisons of Oriental and Western approaches to counseling and guidance.* Paper presented at the annual conference of the Korean Psychological Association, Seoul, Korea.

Lee, E. (1996). Asian American families: An overview. In M. McGoldrick, J. Giordano, & J. Pearce (Eds.), *Ethnicity and family therapy* (pp. 227–248). New York: Guilford Press.

Lee, K. T. (1983). *Koreans' way of thinking.* Seoul, Korea: Sinwon-Moonwhasa.

Maday, B. C., & Szalay, L. B. (1976). Psychological correlates of family socialization in the United States and Korea. In T. Williams (Ed.), *Psychological anthropology* (pp. 45–55). The Hague, The Netherlands: Mouton.

Nichols, M., & Schwartz, R. (1995). *Family and therapy: Concepts and methods.* Boston: Allyn & Bacon.

Shon, S., & Ja, D. (1982). Asian families. In M. McGoldrick, M. Pearce, & J. Giordano (Eds.), *Ethnicity and family therapy* (pp. 208–228). New York: Guilford Press.

Song, S. (1995a, November). *The effects of Korean culture on family relationships*. Paper presented at the Conference of the Korean Association of Family Therapy, Seoul, Korea.

Song, S. (1995b). *Family and family therapy*. Seoul, Korea: Bup Moon Sa.

Tseng, W. S., & Hsu, J. (1991). *Culture, mind and therapy: An introduction to cultural psychiatry*. New York: Brunner/Mazel.

■ ■ ■

PART  III

SPECIAL ISSUES

10

American-Born and Overseas-Born Chinese Americans: Counseling Implications

Y. Barry Chung, PhD
David S. Chou

The Chinese are a major ethnic group among Asian Americans or ethnic minorities in the United States (Wang, 1994). According to the 1990 census data, about 1.65 million Chinese resided in the U.S., double the number reported in the 1980 census. The states of California, New York, and Hawaii are home to about 65% of all Chinese Americans. Approximately 80% of Chinese Americans speak some Chinese at home. Being culturally different, Chinese Americans encounter unique adjustment and mental health issues. Although increased attention has been given to the mental health of Chinese Americans, the special issues facing American-born and overseas-born Chinese Americans are often ignored in the literature. The purpose of this chapter is to discuss variables that differentiate American-born from overseas-born Chinese Americans. Because of the wide range of individual differences, our approach is not to dichotomize Chinese Americans, but to identify variables that are important for understanding the between-groups and within-group differences pertaining to American-born and overseas-born sections of the population. We also suggest some counseling implications pertaining to these populations.

According to Toupin (1980), three major factors must be considered when counseling Asian Americans: (a) time, reason, and destination of immigration; (b) amount and impact of education; and (c) conflicting cultural norms. Furthermore, Chan, Lam, Wong, Leung, and Fang (1988) emphasized the following factors: acculturation, preference of structure in counseling, ways of expressing and verbalizing emotion, and language. For Chinese Americans in particular, Wang (1994) suggested the following variables: place of origin, length of residence in the U.S., education, socioeconomic status (SES), acculturation, interracial marriage, and motivation for counseling. We believe that all of these variables are important for understanding American-born and overseas-born Chinese Americans. Instead of treating them independently, however, we focus on the interrelations of these variables, discussing the educational background; SES; language; acculturation; interracial marriage; political background; and the time, reason, and destination of immigration among Chinese Americans from five major places of birth: Hong Kong, Taiwan, mainland China, Vietnam, and America. Then we address the counseling implications of the variables that account for the between-groups and within-group differences of Chinese Americans.

Five Major Places of Birth

The definitive distinction between American-born and overseas-born Chinese Americans is their place of birth. Chinese people began residing in the U.S. in the 1840s, and most of them were male laborers (Asamen & Berry, 1987). Chin, Lai, and Rouse (1991) reported that in the beginning of this century there were only about 90,000 Chinese in the U.S. because of the Chinese Exclusion Act of 1882 and the National Origins Act of 1924. Since then, there have been three waves of Chinese immigration, resulting from changes in immigration policies (Lee, 1989). The first wave, when the exclusion quotas of Chinese immigrants were lifted in 1965, resulted in a number of middle-class Chinese from Hong Kong, Taiwan, and other Asian countries. The second wave emerged after the Vietnam War in 1975, when Chinese Vietnamese refugees escaped to the U.S. The third wave was a result of a 1979 policy to admit immigrants from mainland China after a 4-decade closed-door policy. Because the three waves of Chinese immigration all happened during the past

35 years, it is not surprising to find that more than 60% of Chinese Americans in the 1990s are overseas-born (Hong & Ham, 1992; Ying, 1990). Lee (1989) suggested that Chinese immigrants are different in country of origin, dialect, political background, migration pattern, SES, and familiarity with the Western culture. Here we will discuss the backgrounds of immigrants from Hong Kong, Taiwan, mainland China, and Vietnam, which are the major places of origin among Chinese immigrants, as well as the background of American-born Chinese persons.

Hong Kong

Hong Kong has undergone major political, economic, and social changes in its 150-year history as a colony of the United Kingdom. Its rapid economic growth since the 1970s has made Hong Kong one of the most economically successful cities in the world. A vast majority of the 6 million residents in Hong Kong are Chinese who speak primarily Cantonese. Because of Hong Kong's political and economic status, however, English is taught as a second language beginning in kindergarten. Young people from Hong Kong often have an English name, making them easily distinguishable from other Chinese immigrants. Because of influences from traditional Chinese culture and international trades, Hong Kong has become a salad bowl that mixes cultures of America, Europe, the Middle East, Japan, and many Asian countries. Lee (1989) suggested that because of the post–World War II rapid growth in light industry and international trade in Hong Kong and Taiwan, young Chinese from these places exhibit a fading of traditional Chinese values. They tend to value autonomy, self-expression, self-assertion, and individual-oriented achievement. On the other hand, Chiu and Kosinski (1995) argued that Hong Kong is still heavily influenced by Confucian and other traditional values despite its rapid development into an international trade center. On the basis of our personal experiences, we concur with Chiu and Kosinski that Hong Kong has successfully achieved an integrated cultural atmosphere by preserving its traditional Chinese culture as well as assimilating other cultures.

A large number of Hong Kong residents have migrated to the U.S. since the 1960s (Lee, 1989). The most common migration reason is to better their quality of life, especially because of the fear of political and economic instability after the return of Hong Kong to mainland China by the United Kingdom on July 1, 1997. Two major clusters of Hong Kong immigrants have emerged. The first group tends to come from lower SES and educational backgrounds. They secure residency in America through their U.S. relatives. With limited English ability, they tend to reside in Chinatown and make their livings in the restaurant or oriental store businesses. The second group tends to have higher SES and educational backgrounds. These immigrants are generally entrepreneurs or international college students who seek employment and U.S. residency after graduation. Being more fluent in English and more acculturated, they are more likely to reside outside of Chinatowns, to hold professional careers, and to have interracial marriages than are the other cluster of Hong Kong immigrants.

Taiwan

Like Hong Kong, Taiwan has also gained drastic economic achievements over the past few decades through international trade. It is different from Hong Kong in several ways. First, because Taiwan is governed by Chinese people, it embraces traditional Chinese values and culture more strongly than does Hong Kong. Second, unlike the salad-bowl cultural atmosphere in Hong Kong, the primary external cultural influences in Taiwan are from Japan and the U.S. Therefore, the Taiwanese have much exposure to and familiarity with American culture. Third, Mandarin and Taiwanese are two major languages spoken in Taiwan, although some young people are not fluent in Taiwanese and some of the older generation may not speak Mandarin. Taiwanese students begin taking English lessons in middle school. Because English is not as commonly used in Taiwan as in Hong Kong, the spoken English of Taiwanese immigrants may not be as fluent as that of Hong Kong immigrants on entry to the U.S.

A large number of Taiwanese have also moved to the U.S. since the 1960s (Lee, 1989). Taiwanese immigrants typically secure permanent residency in the U.S. after obtaining graduate degrees at a U.S. university or because of their international business trades. Their SES and educational levels tend to be high. They are less likely than the Hong Kong immigrants to reside in Chinatowns or to have interracial marriages.

Mainland China

The traditional Chinese values and culture in mainland China were severely challenged during the cultural revolution in 1967 after the Communist party took over the country. Respect for parents, elderly persons, teachers, and cardinal relations was replaced by criticism and attack to ensure total collectivism and selflessness. Zhang (1994) suggested that the submergence of self for the sake of family, community, and country is emphasized in contemporary China. The newer generation is taught Mandarin and the simplified written Chinese, whereas the older generations often speak dialects only. A small number of people with higher education have some exposure to American culture. These people have a better chance to migrate to America by becoming an international student in the U.S.

A number of immigrants from mainland China emerged in the 1980s after the lifting of the closed-door policy in 1979 (Lee, 1989). The Tiananmen Square incident on June 4, 1989, resulted in a much greater number of immigrants leaving China for political reasons. During the past decade, the number of international students from China has surpassed any other country, and many of these students were granted permanent residency in the U.S. Because most of them are highly educated, they often hold professional careers and reside in suburbs rather than in Chinatowns. They typically came from lower SES backgrounds and may need to struggle financially during their studies and the beginning of their careers. In terms of acculturation, immigrants from China are less prepared for Western culture and less fluent in English than are those from Hong Kong and Taiwan. Interracial marriage also seems infrequent.

Vietnam

The Chinese have a history of migration to other Asian countries such as Korea, Vietnam, Malaysia, and Singapore. Many of them managed to preserve their Chinese ethnicity, culture, and language. Although different dialects are spoken in China, the Cantonese dialect seems to be a popular dialect among Chinese Vietnamese.

The Chinese Vietnamese were forced to leave the country as refugees during the Vietnam War. After temporary stays in some countries, many eventually came to the U.S. in the late 1970s (Lee, 1989). Leaving most belongings behind, often including family members, these refugees had to rebuild their lives. Unlike the immigrants from Hong Kong and Taiwan, Chinese Vietnamese refugees were unprepared for migration to the U.S. They may have various educational backgrounds, but their education and vocational skills may not have prepared them well for the American system. Cultural shock and language barriers may cause tremendous hardships. Therefore, many Chinese refugees reside in Chinatowns and make a living in the restaurant or oriental store businesses. Interracial marriage is not common.

American-Born Chinese

American-born Chinese are a heterogeneous group in terms of place of origin. The aforementioned backgrounds of Chinese immigrants from various places are important for understanding their American-born offspring. For example, Palinkas (1982) suggested that Mandarin-speaking Chinese immigrants (e.g., those from Taiwan and mainland China) are usually more educated, financially secure, able to speak English, and ready to accept cultural differences. Therefore, their American-born children are likely to be more educated and acculturated. In addition to language, the variables discussed pertaining to overseas-born Chinese Americans (e.g., education, SES, acculturation, interracial marriage, immigration reason, and political background) should also be considered.

Because American-born Chinese are educated and socialized in the American system, they tend to be more acculturated to the American culture and less identified with the Chinese culture than their overseas-born counterparts. Many American-born Chinese are bilingual, with various degrees of competency in their Chinese language. Because of a lack of practice, the ability to write in Chinese is the exception rather than the rule, and their listening comprehension is usually better than their spoken Chinese. Their Chinese language ability also declines with age, as they have more interactions with English-speaking peers. For those who grow up in Chinatowns, most will move elsewhere when they become independent from their parents. Because of their acculturation level, they are more likely than their overseas-born counterparts to have interracial marriages. The politics of their place of origin concern them less than domestic politics.

Counseling Implications

An understanding of the backgrounds of American-born and overseas-born Chinese Americans is important for counseling professionals working with Chinese clients. Nevertheless, one should not stereotype Chinese American clients on the basis of their place of birth. In this section, we select a few significant variables that account for between-groups and within-group differences among Chinese Americans, and their counseling implications are discussed.

Immigration Experience

The immigration process is a critical experience that may affect virtually every aspect of a person's life. The stress that results from leaving one's country of origin differentiates the American-born from the overseas-born Chinese Americans (Uehara, Takeuchi, & Smukler, 1994). Palinkas (1982) suggested that migration could cause a crisis of identity because of disorganization of the individual's role system and disturbance of identity and self-image. Furthermore, the process of immigration may damage the stability, interpersonal intimacy, and social support provided by a traditional Chinese family structure, which is the major source of support for the Chinese (Yang, 1991). Indeed, Kuo (1976) found that overseas-born Chinese are less mobile, have more Chinese as close friends, are of lower SES, and are less acculturated and adjusted than American-born Chinese. Loo, Tong, and True (1989) also found that overseas-born Chinese reported more depression than American-born Chinese.

When counseling Chinese immigrants, it is important to assess the client's stress related to the immigration experience. Recent immigrants may be particularly vulnerable because of culture shock, language difficulties, differences in educational and vocational training, job search difficulties, trouble finding a home, problems in transportation (e.g., lacking a driver's licence or car), and other basics of living. Instead of focusing on coping with clients' emotions, as in traditional American counseling, it may be more helpful to provide practical assistance, such as workshops (e.g., dealing with cultural differences), and to direct clients to relevant resources (e.g., English classes, educational and vocational training opportunities, job referral services, and apartment locators). A teamwork or outreach approach may be necessary for particular clients.

Palinkas (1982) suggested that Chinatowns and Chinese churches ease the adjustment of Chinese immigrants. On the other hand, a lot of problems are evident in Chinatowns: poverty, unemployment, poor health, suicides, youth gangs, crimes, sweatshops, and identity issues (Sue, Sue, & Sue, 1975). Loo et al., (1989) interviewed Chinese residents of San Francisco's Chinatown. They found that only 5% of respondents had sought mental health services, which was primarily due to a lack of knowledge of services available. Therefore, counselors need to keep Chinese immigrants informed about available mental health services. Another issue of importance in working with Chinese immigrants is language. Lin (1994) found that Chinese American clients stay in psychotherapy with a length comparable with Americans in general when served by therapists matching their ethnicity and language. This finding calls for more bilingual Chinese American counselors.

Acculturation

Leong and Chou (1994) suggested that the ethnic identity of Asian Americans can be conceptualized along two dimensions: attitudes toward one's culture of origin and attitudes toward the mainstream American culture. Those who strongly identify with their own culture but reject the host culture are "separationists." Those who strongly acculturate to the American culture but reject their own culture are "assimilationists." Those who strongly identify with both cultures are "integrationists." Finally, those who reject both cultures are "marginalists," although in reality the emergence of marginalists is infrequent.

A number of interrelated factors influence the acculturation level of Chinese Americans, such as place of birth, age at immigration and length of sojourn, political background, reason for immigration, location of residence in the U.S., SES, education, and language ability. Those who are highly acculturated into the American culture are most likely to be American-born or to have migrated at an early age, to have lived in the U.S. longer, to come from democratic countries, to have migrated for personal-fulfillment purposes, to reside outside of Chinatown, to come from higher SES and educational backgrounds, and to be fluent in English. In light of Leong and Chou's (1994) model, acculturation to the American culture does not necessarily imply alienation from one's own culture. The development of ethnic identity depends on the exposure to the cultures and the interaction of the cultural experiences.

To work effectively with Chinese Americans, counselors need to be familiar with traditional Chinese cultures. It has been well documented that Chinese culture, values, and worldview have been strongly influenced by Confucianism, Taoism, and Buddhism (Ryan, 1985; Yang, 1991). Confucianism is particularly the mainstay of teaching, which places a strong emphasis on a firm hierarchical family structure and male dominance. Five cardinal relations are of central importance in the Confucian teaching: sovereign and subject, father and son, brothers, husband and wife, and friends (Chan et al., 1988). It is important to adhere to the roles expected for each member of the cardinal relations. Asamen and Berry (1987) suggested that age, sex, and generation determine rigid roles undertaken by Chinese family members. To maintain harmony in the family, the Chinese place great emphasis on obedience, control of conduct and emotion, integrity, impulse control, achievement, and acceptance of social obligations rather than on independence, assertiveness, and creativity.

These Chinese values are in sharp contrast to the culture of individualism in the U.S. Therefore, it is important for counselors to adjust their counseling approach according to the ethnic identity of the Chinese client. Furthermore, because the Chinese family is an integral part of every individual, the family system should be taken into account. Lee (1989) suggested that Chinese American families may be classified into four types, according to increasing levels of acculturation. "Traditional families" consist of family members who were all born and raised in Asian countries. They are most likely to strongly identify with their Chinese culture and are least acculturated into the American culture. "Transitional families" consist of parents and grandparents with strong traditional Chinese values and a younger generation that is more westernized. These families often encounter cultural conflicts between the traditional and westernized generations. "Bicultural families" consist of westernized children and their parents who are professional, English speaking, and also westernized. Therefore, conflicts between generations are reduced. Finally, "Americanized families" consist of parents and children who were born and raised in the U.S. These families tend to be least identified with their Chinese culture and most acculturated into mainstream American culture. Counselors need to assess the cultural identity of the family as a whole, as well as that of the individuals. Special attention should be given to cultural conflicts between generations and the involvement of family members in counseling.

Attitudes Toward Counseling

Some recent studies examined factors that affect the Chinese population's motivation for professional help, such as counselor credibility, client acculturation, and problem attribution style. Akutsu, Lin, and Zane (1990) found support for the proximal–distal model, which suggests that an essential component of working with culturally diverse groups is to minimize problems in credibility. The model predicts that counselor credibility is related to continuation in treatment and mediates the influences of cultural knowledge and techniques. Their study suggested that counselor credibility was the best predictor of use intent among both Chinese and White Americans. Counselor approach was also a predictor of use intent among Chinese Americans. Considering the fact that Chinese culture emphasizes authority and hierarchical structure, it seems important to pay particular attention to establishing credibility when working with clients who strongly identify with their traditional Chinese culture. Display of degrees and certificates, professional attire, and assuming an authoritative role may be helpful in that regard.

Tata and Leong (1994) found that Chinese American college students with higher levels of acculturation are more willing to seek psychological help. Similarly, Ying and Miller (1992) found that Chinese Americans who have better skills in English, are younger, and are married and those from lower SES backgrounds tend to have a more positive attitude about help seeking. American-born Chinese are more likely to seek help than overseas-born Chinese. Some of these results may be due to the fact that psychological counseling is largely a Western concept. Individuals with traditional Chinese values may rely more on themselves and support from family and friends in dealing with emotional disturbances. Regarding problem-attribution style, Cheung (1987) found that Chinese patients in Hong Kong who conceptualized their problems in psychological terms were more likely to attempt resolution by turning within, to delay seeking professional help, and to approach mental health professionals rather than physicians when they do seek professional help. Those who attribute their problems to somatic terms were least likely to approach mental health professionals initially but more likely to seek medical solutions. Those who conceptualize their problems in both psychological and physical terms were most likely to seek psychological and psychiatric help early. On the other hand, those who held a physical attribution (i.e., sickness) were more likely to seek medical help. Similarly, Ying (1990) studied a group of recently immigrated Chinese American women and found that those who attributed depression to psychological causes were less likely to seek professional help but would turn within or to family and friends for assistance. Because seeking medical help for physical problems is less likely than seeking psychological help to bring shame to the family, somatization may be common to Chinese Americans with traditional values. To reach out to the less acculturated, it may be helpful to present counseling services in a less threatening way, such as management of physical symptoms and problem solving, rather than labeling them as psychological counseling.

Regarding preference for counseling approach, Yuen and Tinsley (1981) found that American college students expect a less directive and protective counselor, whereas Chinese students expect the counselor to be more directive, nurturing, and authoritative. In two other studies, international Chinese students were found to prefer a directive counseling approach (Exum & Lau, 1988; Mau & Jepsen, 1988). Of course, one should not expect all Chinese clients to prefer directive counseling. The acculturation level of the client needs to be considered along with other individual factors when deciding on a counseling approach.

Interventions

Counselors may consider a variety of interventions when working with overseas-born and American-born Chinese Americans. Modern psychiatry in China began in the 1950s (Xia & Zhang, 1981). Psychotherapy was first provided to patients with neurasthenia or other mental disorders in 1953 (Li, Xu, & Kuang, 1988). A comprehensive treatment approach was designed in 1958 to include three elements: (a) individual and group psychotherapy; (b) drugs and other physical treatments; and (c) *qigong, taijiquan,* and other techniques or martial arts for regulating the body's functioning. The mutual regulation of the mind and body is considered an effective means to maintain harmony with the self and its environment. Researchers and counselors are encouraged to explore the efficacy of traditional Chinese healing methods (e.g., *qigong* and *taijiquan*) in helping recent Chinese immigrants who are less acculturated.

Jung (1984) advocated the use of structural family therapy with Chinese Americans. This is an open systems model that deals with the individual in relation to his or her family and environment. Because of the importance of collectivism in Chinese culture, the social context surrounding the family should be addressed in the counseling process. Lee (1989) suggested that the use of genograms with Chinese family members is successful to examine family migration and relocation history. Readers are encouraged to consult Lee's guidelines for assessment and treatment of Chinese American families.

Hong and Ham (1992) also suggested the use of a family systems approach in working with immigrant Chinese families. There are two major concepts in this theory: morphostasis and morphogenesis. Morphostasis is a regulatory or equilibrium-seeking mechanism that the family uses for maintaining stability, order, and control within the family. Morphogenesis focuses on the growth and development of a family toward greater organizational complexity. The immigrant family strives to maintain stability within the family unit when family members respond to environmental changes and stresses associated with the process of immigration. In this process, the family struggles to maintain a balance of morphostasis and morphogenesis forces. The role of the counselor is to help each family member understand what he or she can do to contribute to a balance of these forces. Therefore, the family system, rather than the individual, becomes the focus of counseling.

Conclusion

In this chapter, we discussed the backgrounds of overseas-born Chinese Americans from Hong Kong, Taiwan, mainland China, and Vietnam, as well as those of American-born Chinese. Counseling implications of some significant variables accounting for between-groups and within-group differences are discussed. Some promising counseling interventions, such as traditional Chinese healing methods and the family systems approach, were also suggested. We encourage counselors to take on a comprehensive approach to understand their Chinese American clients and to provide services that fit their special needs.

References

Akutsu, P. D., Lin, C. H., & Zane, N. W. S. (1990). Predictors of utilization intent of counseling among Chinese and White students: A test of the proximal–distal model. *Journal of Counseling Psychology, 37*, 445–452.

Asamen, J. K., & Berry, G. L. (1987). Self-concept, alienation, and perceived prejudice: Implications for counseling Asian Americans. *Journal of Multicultural Counseling and Development, 15*, 146–160.

Chan, F., Lam, C. S., Wong, D., Leung, P., & Fang, X. (1988). Counseling Chinese Americans with disabilities. *Journal of Applied Rehabilitation Counseling, 19*, 21–25.

Cheung, F. M. (1987). Conceptualization of psychiatric illness and help-seeking behavior among Chinese. *Culture, Medicine and Psychiatry, 11*, 97–106.

Chin, K., Lai, T. M., & Rouse, M. (1991). Social adjustment and alcoholism among Chinese immigrants in New York City. *International Journal of the Addictions, 25*, 709–730.

Chiu, R. K., & Kosinski, F. A. (1995). Chinese cultural collectivism and work-related stress: Implications for employment counselors. *Journal of Employment Counseling, 32*, 98–110.

Exum, H. A., & Lau, E. Y. (1988). Counseling style preference of Chinese college students. *Journal of Multicultural Counseling and Development, 16*, 84–92.

Hong, G. K., & Ham, M. D. (1992). Impact of immigration on the family life cycle: Clinical implications for Chinese Americans. *Journal of Family Psychotherapy*, *3*(3), 27–40.

Jung, M. (1984). Structural family therapy: Its application to Chinese families. *Family Process*, *23*, 365–374.

Kuo, W. (1976). Theories of migration and mental health: An empirical testing on Chinese-Americans. *Social Science and Medicine*, *10*, 297–306.

Lee, E. (1989). Assessment and treatment of Chinese-American immigrant families. *Journal of Psychotherapy and the Family*, *6*, 99–122.

Leong, F. T. L., & Chou, E. L. (1994). The role of ethnic identity and acculturation in the vocational behavior of Asian Americans: An integrative review. *Journal of Vocational Behavior*, *44*, 155–172.

Li, X., Xu, S., & Kuang, P. (1988). 30 years of Chinese clinical psychology. *International Journal of Mental Health*, *16*(3), 3–21.

Lin, J. C. H. (1994). How long do Chinese Americans stay in psychotherapy? *Journal of Counseling Psychology*, *41*, 288–291.

Loo, C., Tong, B., & True, R. (1989). A bitter bean: Mental health status and attitudes in Chinatown. *Journal of Community Psychology*, *17*, 283–296.

Mau, W., & Jepsen, D. A. (1988). Attitudes toward counselors and counseling processes: A comparison of Chinese and American graduate students. *Journal of Counseling and Development*, *67*, 189–192.

Palinkas, L. A. (1982). Ethnicity, identity and mental health: The use of rhetoric in an immigrant Chinese church. *Journal of Psychoanalytic Anthropology*, *5*, 235–258.

Ryan, A. S. (1985). Cultural factors in casework with Chinese-Americans. *Social Casework*, *66*, 333–340.

Sue, S., Sue, D. W., & Sue, D. W. (1975). Asian Americans as a minority group. *American Psychologist*, *30*, 906–910.

Tata, S. P., & Leong, F. T. L. (1994). Individualism–collectivism, social-network orientation, and acculturation as predictors of attitudes toward seeking professional psychological help among Chinese Americans. *Journal of Counseling Psychology*, *41*, 280–287.

Toupin, E. S. W. A. (1980). Counseling Asians: Psychotherapy in the context of racism and Asian-American history. *American Journal of Orthopsychiatry*, *50*, 76–86.

Uehara, E. S., Takeuchi, D. T., & Smukler, M. (1994). Effects of combining disparate groups in the analysis of ethnic differences: Variations among Asian American mental health service consumers in level of community functioning. *American Journal of Community Psychology*, *22*, 83–99.

Wang, L. (1994). Marriage and family therapy with people from China. *Contemporary Family Therapy: An International Journal*, *16*, 25–37.

Xia, Z., & Zhang, M. (1981). History and present status of psychiatry in China. *International Journal of Mental Health*, *16*, 22–29.

Yang, J. (1991). Career counseling of Chinese American women: Are they in limbo? *Career Development Quarterly, 39,* 350–359.

Ying, Y. (1990). Explanatory models of major depression and implications for help-seeking among immigrant Chinese-American women. *Culture, Medicine and Psychiatry, 14,* 393–408.

Ying, Y., & Miller, L. S. (1992). Help-seeking behavior and attitude of Chinese Americans regarding psychological problems. *American Journal of Community Psychology, 20,* 549–556.

Yuen, R. K., & Tinsley, H. E. A. (1981). International and American students' expectancies about counseling. *Journal of Counseling Psychology, 28,* 66–69.

Zhang, W. (1994). American counseling in the mind of a Chinese counselor. *Journal of Multicultural Counseling and Development, 22,* 79–85.

■ ■ ■

11

Ethnic and Sexual Identity Development of Asian American Lesbian and Gay Adolescents

Y. Barry Chung, PhD
Motoni Katayama, EdM

If lesbian and gay people are considered an invisible minority group because they cannot be identified from their physical appearance and because of the oppression and discrimination they encounter, lesbian and gay adolescents may be called the invisible of the invisible. Our society mostly deals with homosexual issues at the adult level as if lesbian and gay adolescents do not exist. Even within the lesbian and gay community, adolescents are not given adequate attention. Resources and services are almost exclusively for adults, possibly because it is too controversial and complex to deal with minors (Savin-Williams, 1990).

Because of a lack of adequate attention and assistance, lesbian and gay adolescents may encounter tremendous difficulty in dealing with their sexual orientation. Problems facing sexual minority youths include feelings of isolation, negative family reaction, ver-

Reprinted from *Professional School Counseling*, volume 1, pages 21–25. Copyright © 1998, The American School Counselor Association.

bal and physical abuse, sexual abuse, sexually transmitted diseases, discrimination, poor school performance, mental health problems, substance abuse, running away, and conflict with the law (Robinson, 1994; Savin-Williams, 1990). It is estimated that lesbian and gay adolescents are two to three times more likely than their heterosexual counterparts to attempt suicide (Rotheram-Borus, Hunter, & Rosario, 1994). In the face of familial and societal neglect and disapproval, school personnel may be the only source of support for lesbian and gay adolescents.

Price and Telljohann's national study (cited in Telljohann & Price, 1993) found that 41% of the school counselors surveyed felt that schools were not making enough effort to assist in the adjustment of lesbian and gay students. Floyd et al. (1995) surveyed 156 teachers, 65 counselors, and 30 administrators of middle and high schools in Michigan. They found that teachers were the most conservative and least informed about lesbian and gay students; counselors were the most supportive, informed, and experienced with these students; and administrators fell somewhere in between. Telljohann and Price's survey also found that about 25% of their lesbian and gay adolescent respondents felt able to discuss sexual identity issues with their school counselors. Therefore, school counselors are in a unique position to take a lead role in the school system to facilitate collaborative efforts with other personnel in helping lesbian and gay students.

Counseling issues pertaining to lesbian and gay adolescents have received increased attention in the literature during the past few years (cf. Robinson, 1994; Rofes, 1994; Rotheram-Borus et al., 1994; Street, 1994; Telljohann & Price, 1993; Uribe & Harbeck, 1992). Yet the impact of ethnicity has been largely ignored in this literature. Bui and Takeuchi (1992) found that Asian Americans are underrepresented in public mental health agencies. This finding may be due to the fact that culturally sensitive services are exceptions rather than the rule. Yeh, Takeuchi, and Sue (1994) found that Asian American children receiving ethnic-specific services were less likely to drop out prematurely, more likely to utilize services, and scored more favorably on outcome measures than those receiving services at mainstream centers. Since American society is becoming more ethnically diverse, multicultural counseling competency becomes more and more important. The purpose of the present article is to discuss the ethnic and sexual identity development and the interaction of the two identities among Asian American lesbian and gay adolescents. These identity development issues are important considerations for counseling this double-minority population.

Ethnic and Sexual Identity Development

Ethnic Identity

Ethnic identity is an important concept in multicultural counseling because of its relation to the psychological well-being of ethnic minority members. In this article, ethnic identity is defined as "one's sense of belonging to an ethnic group and the part of one's thinking, perceptions, feelings, and behavior that is due to ethnic group membership" (Rotheram & Phinney, 1987, p. 13). Since Cross (1971) proposed a model delineating the ethnic identity development of Black Americans, other models have been suggested for other ethnic groups (cf. Atkinson, Morten, & Sue, 1979; Berry, 1980; D. W. Sue & Sue, 1990; S. Sue & Sue, 1973).

D. W. Sue and Sue's (1990) Ethnic Identity Development Model consists of four stages: (a) conformity, the person identifies with the majority cultural group and devalues his/her own ethnic group; (b) dissonance, conflicts arise between one's attitudes toward the majority group and one's own ethnic group; (c) resistance/immersion, the person identifies with his/her ethnic group and devalues the majority cultural group; and (d) integrative awareness, the person realizes that every culture has its strengths and weaknesses and opposes all forms of racism.

Some other models focus on ethnic identity attitudes without suggesting linear developmental stages. Ethnic identity attitudes are cognitive and emotional reactions toward one's own ethnic group and toward the majority group as a result of intercultural contact and group relations (Berry, 1989; Berry, Kim, Power, Young, & Bujaki, 1989). According to Berry, ethnic minority persons may be classified into four modes of acculturation: (a) assimilation, valuing the majority culture over one's own culture; (b) separation, preserving one's culture while withdrawing from the majority culture; (c) marginalization, losing cultural contact and identification with one's culture as well as the majority culture; and (d) integration, valuing and integrating one's culture as well as the majority culture.

The models cited above share some important themes. First, ethnic identity pertains to a person's attitudes toward his/her cultural group and the majority cultural group. Second, these attitudes are developed through an acculturation process and are results of interracial relations. Experiences of racism, oppression, and discrimination play an important role in this developmental process. Third, an integrated ethnic identity is considered to be most desirable.

Sexual Identity

Anderson's (1994) review of research on adult lesbians and gay males suggests that awareness of same-sex feelings and attractions occurs during adolescence. Same-sex activities begin during early to mid-adolescence for gay males and around the age of 20 for lesbians. In a survey of 13 Japanese American gay men, Wooden, Kawasaki, and Mayeda (1983) found that about half of them began to have same-sex feelings in their early teens, whereas others began in their late teens or early twenties.

Findings from retrospective research with adult participants are consistent with studies that involve adolescent participants. Telljohann and Price (1993) surveyed 120 lesbian and gay adolescents and found that both sexes became aware of their sexual orientation between the ages of 4 and 18. Uribe and Harbeck (1992) interviewed lesbian and gay adolescents and reported an average age of 14 for the onset of same-sex experience for gay males, whereas such experience seemed to occur much later among lesbians. These findings coincide with Anderson's (1994) conclusion that gay males tend to engage in same-sex activities earlier than lesbians.

Evidently, adolescence marks the beginning of one's awareness and exploration of homosexual orientation. This journey may involve feelings of confusion, shame, and fear. A suspected or disclosed homosexual orientation may lead to isolation, rejection, humiliation, harassment, or physical assault. Uribe and Harbeck (1992) found that many individuals assumed to be homosexual were harassed by teachers and peers in elementary school and such experience intensified in secondary school.

A few models have been proposed to delineate the sexual identity development of lesbians and gay males. The homosexual identity development model proposed by Cass (1979) includes six stages: (a) identity confusion, the person feels confused because his/her awareness of same-sex attraction is in conflict with his/her previously assumed heterosexual orientation; (b) identity comparison, the person feels different and alienated from others; (c) identity tolerance, the person tolerates his/her increasing emotional and behavioral affiliation with a homosexual identity; (d) identity acceptance, the person accepts homosexual orientation as an alternative identity; (e) identity pride, the person devalues heterosexuality and takes pride in being homosexual; and (f) identity synthesis, the person integrates his/her homosexual identity with other identities and appreciates sexual-orientation diversity.

Another model was proposed by Troiden (1989) and includes four stages: (a) sensitization, the person becomes sensitive of being different from his/her same-sex peers in terms of sex-role behaviors and sexual feelings; (b) identity confusion, the person feels confused about his/her sexual identity because of increasing awareness of same-sex feelings that are incongruent with his/her previously assumed heterosexual orientation and because of ignorance and inaccurate knowledge about homosexuality; (c) identity assumption, this stage is characterized by identity tolerance and acceptance, experimentation of same-sex experience, and getting involved in the lesbian and gay community; and (d) commitment, the person sustains a positive homosexual identity and engages in a committed same-sex love relationship.

The above models are similar in that they both consider the formation of sexual identity as a developmental process in which a person progresses in the following order: awareness of same-sex feelings, feeling confused because one's assumed sexual orientation differs from one's perceived orientation, tolerance and acceptance of a lesbian or gay identity, and integration of sexual identity with other aspects of life. However, both Cass and Troiden agreed that this development may not be a linear stage-by-stage process because of individual differences. The developmental process is largely dependent on the interaction between the individual and the environment (Cass, 1979). Encounters of heterosexism, homophobia, oppression, and discrimination are major determinants in how the developmental process unfolds.

Interrelations Between Ethnic and Sexual Identity Attitudes

Homosexuality in Asian Cultures

There is not much qualitative difference between Asian and American cultures in terms of traditional attitudes toward homosexuality, but the intensity of heterosexism and homophobia is much stronger in Asian cultures than in the American culture. Traditional Asian cultures emphasize rules of nature, harmony with nature and people, and complementarity. For example, "Yin–Yang" is a key concept of harmony and complementarity in China. Many other Asian cultures, such as Korea and Japan, endorse a similar concept. Yin–Yang represents night and day, cold and warm, negative and positive, female and male, and the like. It signifies the complementarity of two contrasting entities. The concept of Yin–Yang determines that a person should be unified with a person of the opposite sex. Therefore, homosexuality is against nature.

Chan (1989) suggested that being homosexual in Asian cultures is in conflict with the traditional gender roles for men (continuation of the family) and women (taking care of husband and children). Because traditional gender roles and the family system are central to most Asian cultures, violation of gender roles and threats to the family system are unacceptable. Consequently, homosexuality is censored.

There are other reasons why homosexuality is not accepted in Asian cultures. Many modern Asian countries developed out of agricultural societies which relied primarily on human labor. The larger a family, the more human power and economic potential. In addition, inheritance of family property was often determined by the number of children (usually males). Therefore, men and women traditionally have been expected to get married and have many children so that they can inherit more property and secure greater human power and economic status. Homosexuality works against this economic tradition and, therefore, is not acceptable.

Because heterosexism and homophobia are so intense in Asian cultures, an openly homosexual lifestyle is often not an option. The consequence of disclosing one's sexual orientation is just too threatening. Therefore, lesbians and gay men in many Asian societies are almost totally *invisible*. In such an environment, lesbian and gay youths deal with their sexual orientation without any assistance. There is no organization or role model to help them develop a lesbian or gay identity. Most individuals suppress their sexual orientation and follow expectations of a heterosexual lifestyle, although there might be some discreet homosexual activities. Most lesbian and gay Asians eventually get married and have children. Consequently, in many Asian cultures there is no such concept as a lesbian or gay identity.

Asians in American Gay Culture

The American lesbian and gay community seems to be more accepting of ethnic diversity than the mainstream American culture. Interracial same-sex couples are relatively common. Nevertheless, Newman and Muzzonigro (1993) suggested that the lesbian and gay community is still predominantly White and middle-class oriented and is not responsive to ethnic minorities. Wooden et al.'s

(1983) Japanese American gay male respondents reported being discriminated against and stereotyped by other gay men. Chan's (1989) Asian American lesbian and gay respondents also reported being stereotyped and unacknowledged by the larger homosexual community.

Asian Americans may feel rejected by the lesbian and gay community because they are often considered sexually unattractive. On the other hand, they may be actively pursued by a small group of people who are particularly attracted to Asians. It seems difficult for Asian Americans to be seen as unique individuals beyond the overshadowing factor of ethnicity. Fitting in the majority lesbian and gay community could be a frustrating experience.

Interaction of Ethnic and Sexual Identity Attitudes

On the basis of the above discussion, we suggest that the developments of ethnic and sexual identity attitudes are interactive among Asian American lesbians and gay males. This argument is based on two rationales. The first rationale is that the development of an integrated Asian American ethnic identity and the development of an integrated lesbian or gay identity involve parallel psychological processes. More specifically, the development of an integrated ethnic identity involves (a) acceptance of one's cultural heritage and other cultures, (b) understanding of racism and discrimination, and (c) integrating ethnic identity with other identities. The development of an integrated lesbian or gay identity involves (a) acceptance of one's sexual orientation and the orientations of others, (b) understanding of heterosexism and discrimination, and (c) integrating sexual identity with other identities. The two psychological processes are parallel and signify the double-minority status of Asian American lesbians and gay males.

Our second rationale is that the ethnic and sexual identity attitudes of Asian American sexual minorities are interrelated. While American culture is far from affirmative of homosexual orientation, it is relatively more tolerant in dealing with sexual minorities when compared with Asian cultures. Furthermore, because the American lesbian and gay community is White and middle-class oriented, trying to fit in this community involves dealing with one's ethnicity. Those who strongly endorse their traditional Asian culture and beliefs are likely to face barriers in developing a positive lesbian or gay identity because of their culture's rejection of homosexuality. On the other hand, those who strongly identify with the American lesbian and gay culture may have problems dealing with their Asian identity because of racism and the overshadowing factor of ethnicity. A positive Asian American lesbian or gay identity cannot be achieved without effectively dealing with one's double-minority status. Such effort involves the parallel psychological processes of developing integrated ethnic and sexual identities.

Counseling Implications

School counselors often work in a conservative setting with various administrative and political constraints. Provision of counseling services for Asian American lesbian and gay students may face resistance from administrators, teachers, parents, and even counselors themselves. Floyd et al. (1995) reported that 22.5% of the teachers, 20% of the administrators, and 15.7% of the counselors surveyed considered homosexuality offensive for religious reasons. In addition to heterosexism and homophobia, racism and racial stereotypes are also barriers to effective counseling. Counselors need to examine their attitudes and deal with their biases before they can effectively work with Asian American lesbian and gay students.

The development of positive ethnic and sexual identities is important to the psychological well-being of Asian American lesbians and gay males. Adolescence marks the beginning of this critical process. The role of the school counselor is to help these students develop an integrated Asian American lesbian or gay identity. First, it is important to assess the student's ethnic and sexual identity attitudes. The identity development models discussed in this article are helpful for assessing such attitudes. The counselor needs to pay attention to the interaction between the student's ethnic and sexual identity attitudes (that is, how ethnic identity attitudes affect sexual identity attitudes and vice versa). As discussed earlier, the two identity development processes are parallel and interrelated. We suggest that counselors may take advantage of the parallel psychological processes in helping students to develop their ethnic and sexual identities. Interventions for the two identity domains may be utilized simultaneously, although sometimes an individual may be more ready to deal with one identity than the other. The counselor needs to adjust to the readiness of the student and help the student connect the two identity domains so that progress in one domain can be mirrored in another. The final goal is the integration of ethnic and sexual identities with other identities.

One critical issue in the coming out process for Asian Americans is familial reaction. Newman and Muzzonigro (1993) found that gay male adolescents from more-traditional families felt more disapproval of their sexual orientation than gay males from less-traditional families. Wooden et al. (1983) found that most of their Japanese American gay male respondents had come out to their friends, but only about half of them had come out to their families. Considering Asian families' possible traditional values, counselors need to help students assess their family's attitudes toward homosexuality before making decisions about coming out. Because adolescents are emotionally and financially dependent, oftentimes the best decision is to postpone coming out to family members.

Finally, another important issue for counseling Asian American lesbian and gay adolescents is their sexual experience exploration. American adolescents are at risk for sexually transmitted diseases (STDs) because of engagement in unprotected sex due to a lack of knowledge or irrational beliefs that they can remain free from STDs. Compared with other ethnic groups, Asian Americans tend to be more conservative about sex. For example, Chinese Americans have been found to be more conservative sexually than White Americans in terms of their age of first sexual experience, percentage of people engaging in premarital sex, and percentage of people who are sexually active (Huang, 1994; Strunin, 1991). On the other hand, because sex is a taboo subject in many Asian cultures, Asian American adolescents may be less knowledgeable about STDs. Indeed, Strunin's (1991) research found that, among four ethnic groups (Asian, Black, Hispanic, and White), Asian American adolescents were least knowledgeable of AIDS. Therefore, STDs and AIDS education should be an emphasis in counseling Asian American lesbian and gay adolescents.

Conclusion

In this article, a theory of the ethnic and sexual identity development of Asian American lesbian and gay adolescents is proposed. It is suggested that the two identity development processes are parallel and interactive. Although counseling implications are offered, this theory remains to be tested empirically. Furthermore, the model may be applicable to other ethnic minorities. Research in this area is strongly encouraged.

References

Anderson, D. A. (1994). Lesbian and gay adolescents: Social and developmental considerations. *High School Journal, 77*(1/2), 13–19.

Atkinson, D. R., Morten, G., & Sue, D. W. (1979). *Counseling American minorities.* Dubuque, IA: William C. Brown.

Berry, J. W. (1980). Acculturation as varieties of adaptation. In A. M. Padilla (Ed.), *Acculturation: Theory, models and some new findings* (pp. 9–25). Boulder, CO: Westview Press.

Berry, J. W. (1989). Psychology of acculturation. In J. Berman (Ed.), *Nebraska symposium on motivation* (Vol. 37, pp. 201–234). Lincoln: University of Nebraska Press.

Berry, J. W., Kim, U., Power, S., Young, M., & Bujaki, M. (1989). Acculturation attitudes in plural societies. *Applied Psychology: An International Review, 38*, 185–206.

Bui, K. T., & Takeuchi, D. T. (1992). Ethnic minority adolescents and the use of community mental health care services. *American Journal of Community Psychology, 20*(4), 403-417.

Cass, V. C. (1979). Homosexuality identity formation: A theoretical model. *Journal of Homosexuality, 4*, 219-235.

Chan, C. S. (1989). Issues of identity development among Asian-American lesbians and gay men. *Journal of Counseling and Development, 68*, 16–20.

Cross, W. E. (1971). Negro-to-Black conversion experience: Toward a psychology of Black liberation. *Black World, 20*, 13–17.

Floyd, F. J., Thome, M., VerBeek, T., Sebulske, F., Wolfe, M., & Leacock, K. (1995, August). *School teachers', counselors', and administrators' attitudes regarding lesbian/gay students.* Paper presented at the American Psychological Association Annual Convention, New York.

Huang, L. N. (1994). An integrative approach to clinical assessment and intervention with Asian-American adolescents. *Journal of Clinical Child Psychology, 1*, 21–31.

Newman, B. S., & Muzzonigro, P. G. (1993). The effects of traditional family values on the coming out process of gay male adolescents. *Adolescence, 28*, 213–226.

Robinson, K. E. (1994). Addressing the needs of gay and lesbian students: The school counselor's role. *School Counselor, 41*, 326–332.

Rofes, E. E. (1994). Making our schools safe for sissies. *High School Journal, 77*(1/2), 37–40.

Rotheram, M., & Phinney, J. (1987). Definitions and perspectives in the study of children's ethnic socialization. In J. Phinney & M. Rotheram (Eds.), *Children's ethnic socializations: Pluralism and development* (pp. 10–28). Newbury Park, CA: Sage.

Rotheram-Borus, M. J., Hunter, J., & Rosario, M. (1994). Suicidal behavior and gay-related stress among gay and bisexual male adolescents. *Journal of Adolescent Research, 9*(4), 498–508.

Savin-Williams, R. C. (1990). Gay and lesbian adolescents. *Marriage and Family Review, 14*(3/4), 197–216.

Street, S. (1994). Adolescent male sexuality issues. *School Counselor, 41*, 319–325.

Strunin, L. (1991). Adolescents' perceptions of risk for HIV infection: Implications for future research. *Social Science and Medicine, 32*(2), 221–228.

Sue, D. W., & Sue, D. (1990). *Counseling the culturally different: Theory and practice.* New York: Wiley.

Sue, S., & Sue, D. W. (1973). Chinese-American personality and mental health. In S. Sue & N. N. Wagner (Eds.), *Asian Americans: Psychological perspectives* (pp. 111–124). Palo Alto, CA: Science & Behavior Books.

Telljohann, S. K., & Price, J. H. (1993). A qualitative examination of adolescent homosexuals' life experiences: Ramifications for secondary school personnel. *Journal of Homosexuality, 26*(1), 41–56.

Troiden, R. (1989). The formation of homosexual identities. *Journal of Homosexuality, 17*(1/2), 43–73.

Uribe, V., & Harbeck, K. M. (1992). Addressing the needs of lesbian, gay, and bisexual youth: The origins of Project 10 and school-based intervention. *Journal of Homosexuality, 22*(3/4), 9–28.

Wooden, W. S., Kawasaki, H., & Mayeda, R. (1983). Lifestyles and identity maintenance among gay Japanese-American males. *Alternative Lifestyles, 5*(4), 236–243.

Yeh, M., Takeuchi, D. T., & Sue, S. (1994). Asian-American children treated in the mental health system: A comparison of parallel and mainstream outpatient service centers. *Journal of Clinical Child Psychology, 1*, 5–12.

■ ■ ■

12

The Practice of Family Therapy With Asian Families: A Conversation With Insoo Kim Berg

Kit S. Ng, PhD

Insoo Kim Berg, MSSW, a native of Korea, balances her Eastern heritage with her Western training in her clinical practice and teaching. She is director of the Brief Family Therapy Center in Milwaukee, Wisconsin, is the author of *Working With the Problem Drinker* (with Scott Miller; 1992), and *Family Preservation and Family-Based Services: A Solution-Focused Approach* (1994). Insoo has published more than 20 journals and conducted numerous workshops for mental health professionals around the globe. In the following interview, Insoo converses on issues relating to Asian families, cultural norms, treatment issues, and training Asian therapists.

Ng: A few years ago, you wrote an article called "Different and Same: Family Therapy With Asian-American Families" published in the *Journal of Marriage and Family Therapy*. How did you come out with those ideas? Can you elaborate on how the concept on "Different and Same" works with Asian families?

Berg: I believe that Asian families are so different in terms of their religion, language, education, ethics, and belief systems. I want to point out that there are indeed significant differences on a macrolevel. In some ways, we are the same in that we want to be validated, respected, and we all want to be able to say that what I am doing is okay. This is especially true of Asian families. I would call it a common denominator, which is their sameness.

Ng: What are the significant differences you see within the macrolevel?

Berg: I think the issue of language is significant at the microlevel. I'm increasingly thinking from the linguistic point of view. It's just the basic ways of conceptualizing the language. It forces us to think in terms of the meaning language has in our life and culture. You know, in the West, the emphasis is heavy on "I" rather than "we." The whole social system, legal system, treatment system, and political system are leaning toward "I," whereas the Asian mind-set thinks in terms of "we." I think it creates significant differences at all levels.

Ng: You mentioned the microsystem. I wonder, what significant differences do you see in the microsystem within the Asian families?

Berg: I think that at the microlevel there are a lot of differences, depending on social class. For example, there is a lot of difference between the upper and lower class. I think the cultural difference between the classes are very distinct. Therefore, whether you are a Chinese American, Korean American, or Japanese American, the cultural differences are there within the same culture. To give an example, in Singapore and Hong Kong, class differences are very significant.

Ng: Highlighting the differences has its limited value. Can you comment on the functions of sameness at the microlevel?

Berg: Going back to working with Asian families, the family is a very significant unit and vital social fabric in Asian cultures. I think that both cultures (Western and Asian) value the sameness very much. Sameness tends to draw and tie us together. I am referring to such elements as wanting to be respected, loved, and cared for, whether within the family or for the individual. I think that's the basic similarity. How we try to achieve these basic human needs is a different topic. I think the different ways to achieve these elements is where the differences come in. I think this is where you can draw the distinction between sameness and difference between the Western and Eastern culture.

Ng: What are some myths and realities of Asian families that are often perceived by other subcultures?

Berg: A lot of non-Asians have their stereotypes of Asian families. For example, they think that all Asian families are destined to go to Ivy League schools and that all Asians are gifted in math and science. I think those myths came about because of the gap in the language proficiency. It's easier to study math than psychology (for Asians) or clinical practice (i.e., family therapy). Using verbal skills and developing proficiency in the English language has not been traditionally encouraged by Asians. I think we are seeing some gradual changes in this area. Quite a few Asians have gone into the helping profession, and a lot more second-generation Asians or immigrants are coming into human services. So, I think that as Asians become more comfortable with the subtle nuances of language, they will take more risks to explore the helping profession.

Ng: There have been a lot of discussions and writings on foreign-born and American-born Asians. How difficult is it for non-Asians to understand the difference between foreign-born and American-born Asians? Can you provide some clarifications on this matter?

Berg: Our children are American-born. I think the school system, which is the major catalyst of our cultural values, has a partial responsibility to help bridge the cultural gap between immigrants and American-born Asians. Children born here tend to have different sets of values from their parents. They often experience a cultural clash as evidenced from some of my clinical work with them. One of the major differences is that parents have a certain image of the children when they grow up here. And the parents are very unaware of this image that they have of their children. The children, on the other hand, have a hard time conforming to this parental image. Then there's a clash, and often they do not know how to deal with it. The parents from foreign countries definitely do not have the skills to deal with this kind of conflict. When their children disagree with them, they don't know how to handle it as an adult because they have not seen this and have no experience dealing with parent–child conflict resolution. Most immigrant parents do not have to deal with disrespectful children demanding their rights in Asia because children are expected to respect and obey parental rules without questions.

Ng: The notion seems to be that Asian cultures are very structured and hierarchical. I feel that this is one of the core issues with which Asian families are struggling here. How do you bridge a structured culture with a Western culture that seems to emphasize freedom, individualism, and personal rights?

Berg: I think that there is no easy answer to this question. Often these are two conflicting entities. What I can tell is that in the overall structure there's a lot of change at the microlevel. On the other hand, at the macrolevel, some definite structures exist. It is hard to cross the boundaries here. I think it's nice that Asian families have an overall macrostructure. Once you know what the boundaries are, you have a lot of freedom within the boundaries. This really fascinates me.

Ng: You have done some work with Asian families. What are some outstanding concerns or needs they have to deal with in therapy?

Berg: I think one of the major concerns is that of family conflict. It often spills over into the different social systems, like domestic violence cases. Here the rules are clear on domestic violence, but in Asia the rules are not clear. Family members have to relearn some of these rules in a hard way. The differences are very substantial. In cases of child abuse, Asians sometimes bump against the social rules and legal systems here in America. They have no experience in coping with that. In a lot of cases, all the family members are affected when the legal systems are involved with the perpetuator and the victim. As long as they don't clash with this kind of law, they can stay model citizens. But I think that when they bump against the legal system, it perpetuates severe stress, and a lot of immigrant families have to learn new skills to deal with it, and in most cases it's too late.

Ng: It seems that the clashes have to do with the different cultural norms and mores that we mentioned earlier.

Berg: Yes, indeed. I see that in Asian countries such as Japan. What they call "truancy," Americans call "school refusal." It is absolutely inconceivable to Japanese that students have taken on themselves to decide not go to school. Asian families in America find it extremely embarrassing, unthinkable, and frustrating if their children refuse to go to school. And they are just absolutely baffled by reports of boys beating up their mothers. This really challenged the long-held belief system of respecting the elderly for generations. If they do not find resourceful ways of handling all of these, that's when they seem to come for therapy. Family therapy seems to be a viable way to deal with some of these concerns effectively.

Parents would do anything for their children and will come for family therapy for the sake of the kids. I think that family therapy would be very popular in many of these Asian countries, as well as for Asian families here.

Ng: Let's say an Asian family in the U.S. needs help. Do such families tend to look for Asian or non-Asian therapists?

Berg: I'm not sure if I can be definite about this. They seem to go to both. Some families, when they look for professional help, prefer professionals from their own culture. It has a lot to do with the language issue. When they cannot adequately express themselves, then they tend to look for Asian therapists, but if they are fluent with the language, they tend to look for non-Asian therapists. The issue of privacy is one of the main concerns here. If they are part of the Asian community, let's say the Korean community, they are afraid that news would lead out that they are getting therapy. They do not want people to know that they are in therapy, to avoid any gossip. In my experience, I found that the families I worked with will tell me a lot of things because I'm not hooked up with any Korean community. So I think they like the privacy and my ability to speak Korean. This has been really helpful to the families.

Ng: What treatment approaches do you find to be most helpful for Asian families?

Berg: Well, most Asian families would not do well in long-term therapy. They want results right away. In this aspect, Asian families do not seem to have patience. They are very result oriented. I think they expect the therapy to help them solve the presented problems. They want to get on with their normal life as quickly as possible. This is true across the board for Asian families.

Ng: I understand that Asian families are so different in their own ways. For a therapist who has no experience working with Asian families, what are some of the cultural issues that the therapist need to consider?

Berg: I think the first crucial point is to understand the Eastern norm of "saving face." This long-held belief is for children to save face for their parents. It is not acceptable to humiliate, insult, or blame the parents. And this is very different from Western culture. Asians highly endorse respecting their elders for generations. This is essential. This is also a very strong obligation within the family system. Individualism is very foreign to the Asian mind-set. Therefore, a child having problems is often perceived as a failure of the family unit as a whole.

Ng: In one of your articles, you advocated the notion that it is okay to work with Asian families if you are not Asian. Can you comment on that?

Berg: Well, the number of immigrants has increased sharply the past decade, and there are just not enough Asian therapists. For example, in Los Angeles, there is such a huge Korean population, with very few Korean-speaking therapists. So, for purely practical purposes, Asian families will have to get services from non-Asian therapists.

Ng: Can you talk about the solution-focused approach working with Asian families?

Berg: Of course, I'm biased, very biased in talking about solution-focused therapy (SFT). Nevertheless, I'm going to offer my biased opinion. First of all, I think SFT emphasizes listening and respecting the client and also helps clients to seek solutions in their lives. This is why I really like this approach. The therapist carefully listens to the client and the client eventually guides the process. It is the notion of leading from one step behind, rather than standing in front and trying to pull someone. This not-knowing posture is really powerful. The client is deemed as the expert on his or her own issues. The crucial piece is a matter of respecting the cultural differences rather than eliminating them. This is a way of trying to preserve the culture of the client and also respect what the client brings to the new culture. In a way, it is impossible for the therapist to know all the different nuances of every immigrant group and the complex social class differences in the same groups. I think SFT helps to define the client's cultural identity.

Ng: What are some of the specific theoretical elements of SFT that seem to have appeal for Asian families?

Berg: Yes. Many people have expressed to me that SFT is very Eastern. I agree because many of the original ideas of SFT are very similar to Buddhism, such as the concept of change. Change in SFT is dynamic and not static. Change occurs all the time. Nothing is stable, and this is derived from the Buddha's notion of change. I believe that therapists, in essence, do not create change. Most important, therapists support the change that clients are experiencing, rather than pushing and pulling clients. I feel that we can go with the force of change that the client is capable of, very much like martial arts.

Ng: Well, part of our conversation seems to focus on the need for trained Asian therapists. What do you see as the future of family therapy (with Asian families) and Asian therapists in America?

Berg: I think the obvious thing to do is to highlight the needs of Asian communities in regard to mental health. Society in general lives with the myth that Asians are very hard working and they are the model minority. We have our own community and family problems, such as juvenile delinquency, violence in the home, and job stress. These problems are often swept under the rug. My sense is that the need for services among Asians will continue to grow. I think one of the things that can help promote the field of mental health and attract more Asians is basically to educate the Asian community concerning the myths of mental health. I feel an urgent need for experienced Asian therapists to be mentors to those who aspire to be therapists.

Ng: I'd like to thank you for taking the time for this interview.

Berg: I enjoyed it.

■ ■ ■